C. & T. Harris (Calne)
An Illustrated History

DEE LA VARDERA

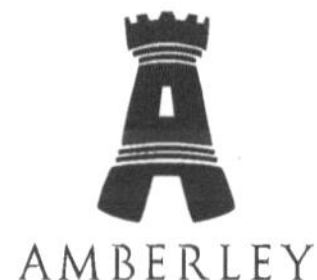

AMBERLEY

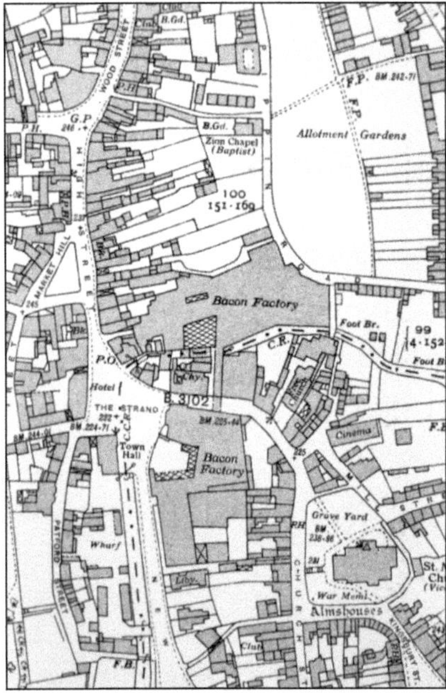

OS map of Calne, 1936. (Wiltshire and Swindon History Centre)

First published 2022

Amberley Publishing
The Hill, Stroud,
Gloucestershire, GL5 4EP

www.amberley-books.com

ISBN: 978 1 3981 0848 6 (print)
ISBN: 978 1 3981 0849 3 (ebook)

British Library Cataloguing in Publication Data.
A catalogue record for this book is available from the British Library.

Typeset in 10pt on 13pt Celeste.
Typesetting by SJmagic DESIGN SERVICES, India.
Printed in the UK.

Contents

Introduction

Calne is a very different place today from the one described by R. N. Worth in his 1887 book *Tourists' Guide to Wiltshire: Its Scenery and Antiquities.*

> Calne has been fortunate in its business relations. Its cloth trade is now extinct but it flourishes by the production of 'Wiltshire Bacon' and may be termed the Cincinnati of England. Many thousands of swine are slaughtered, and cured in Calne annually in the two large factories.

Cincinnati, nicknamed 'Porkopolis', was the pork capital of the United States, sitting on the Ohio River. Calne, considerably smaller, sitting on the River Marden – a small tributary of the Avon – was highly regarded worldwide for its quality pork products. Just as the meat processing industry declined in Cincinnati, so it did too in Calne.

Calne was not alone in being a one-industry town in north Wiltshire: Westinghouse, Chippenham, Avon Rubber, Melksham, and the Ministry of Defence in Corsham are examples. There were economic effects and long-term consequences from closures in such towns.

C. & T. Harris closed in 1982, leaving behind 212 years of meat processing tradition. The buildings were demolished and the site cleared in 1984–86. There was nothing to show that there had ever been such a monumental enterprise in the town. Gone the towering presence of the factory. Gone the noise, the smell, and the relentless activity.

You will never again see pigs running loose on the streets of Calne or crowds of workers swarming out from their shifts, or large refrigerated lorries holding up traffic as they manoeuvre from the dispatch yard onto The Strand. Never again.

The town centre today is unrecognisable, with its colourful spring and summer floral displays, riverside shops and café, award-winning library, sculptures, pop-up pocket park, and arts and nature trails. New housing estates and schools have sprung up over the years; small businesses drawn to the industrial park; independent shops and supermarkets opening – all bringing new life to the town. The population increased from 10,289 in 1981 to 18,408 in 2019.

We need to remember the past to understand and appreciate the present – the milestones and the stumbling blocks that have marked the way.

Calne Heritage Centre archives, housed in the old Carnegie Library, built on land given by the Harris family, holds collections of photographs, documents and artefacts, which record the history of Calne and surrounding area. It is time to open up the albums and turn the pages of time to remind us what working life at C. & T. Harris (Calne) Ltd was like, and how a meat processing factory and its workers contributed to the town's already rich and varied history.

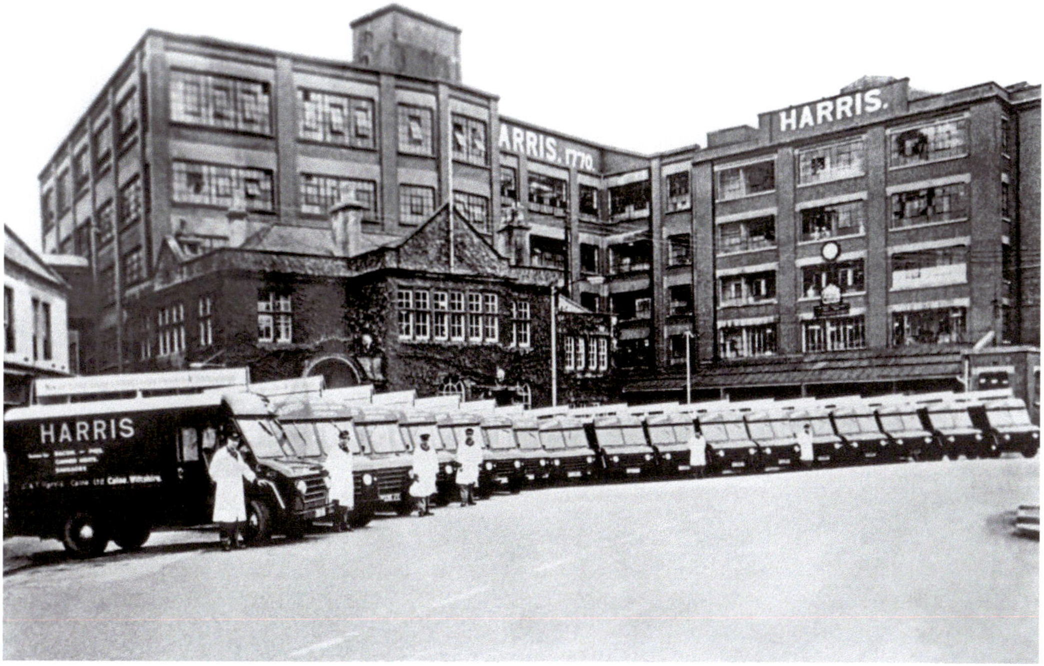

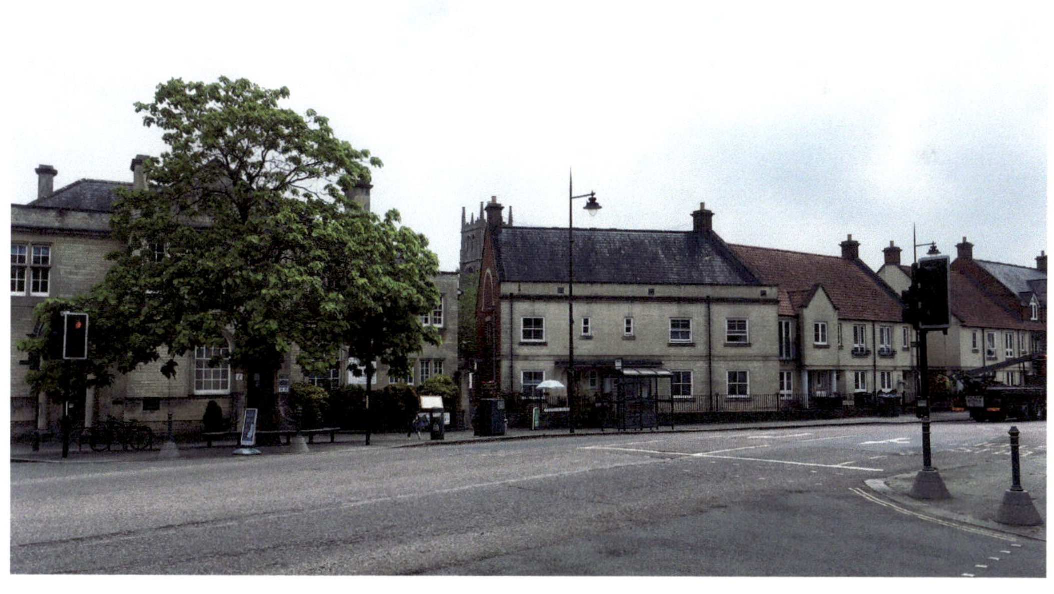

Harris fleet of Commer vans on The Strand, late 1960s. Bank House is on the left.

The same view in 2020. A tree is now in front of Bank House, and Carnegie Mews has been built on the Harris factory site along New Road.

The Harris Family Businesses, 1770–1899

'The Name HARRIS is our distinctive and exclusive Brand, Name and Trademark.
It is our guarantee, and your safeguard.'

Many successful businesses started small, quite often the brainchild of one person, often from a humble background. So it was with widow Sarah Harris, who moved from Devizes to Calne in 1770 with her ten-year-old son John. She opened a pork butcher's shop in Church Street, in the part formerly called Butcher Row. As he grew older, John took on more responsibilities and the business thrived. He married local girl Ann Cotton, and they had three sons – John, and twins James and Henry. John senior died in 1791, aged thirty-one, and his widow continued looking after the business with her children. 'She thought it a good week if she had killed five or six pigs and sold clear out on a Saturday night,' Harriet Cooper wrote in her *Family History of the Harris Family* in 1907.

In 1805–06, son John opened another butcher's shop at the corner of the High Street where he cured bacon and made other pork products. When Ann Harris died in 1809, aged fifty, she left £180 (equivalent to £14,634 today) to be divided among her three sons.

John junior married Mary Perkins and they had eleven children – most of whom became involved in the family business. In 1813, his brother Henry married Mary's sister, Sophia Perkins. The Perkins family ran a family grocers and bakery in Butcher Row, and after the deaths of the parents, they took over the business, adding bacon curing and changing the name to Harris. Henry continued to run the Butcher Row shop and was recorded as a 'baker and bacon factor'.

Henry and Sophia adopted four of John and Mary Harris's eleven children: John (three), Henry junior, James and George. Of the remaining seven children of John and Mary, it was brothers Charles and Thomas who took over the High Street shop. After their father's early death from tuberculosis, in 1837, widow Mary continued to run the business, eventually handing it over to her two sons. The range of produce grew, with pork pies proving to be a very successful line, continuing to be a great favourite in the future story of Harris products. Bacon, however, was always king.

In the early nineteenth century, Wiltshire's reputation for producing superior bacon was growing; the name was a guarantee of high quality. Wiltshire bacon had been prepared in a particular way: the pig's carcase singed after slaughter, the hair, feet, head, offal, intestines, tail, and backbone removed, the two sides separated and then separately cured intact.

The method of curing bacon developed by the Harris family around 1843 became the 'Wiltshire Cure'. Carcases were first injected with a mixture of salt and saltpetre – potassium nitrate, a mineral which could be found locally in soil and rock. They had another coating of the same mixture and were stacked for twenty-one days. The resulting product was very salty. The process needed a cool atmosphere so it could only be carried out in winter months, the salt acting as the preservative through the warmer months.

Before the railways, pigs imported from southern Ireland arrived at Bristol from Cork, and were taken by road to market in London. Calne's position on the main coaching route from London to Bristol proved advantageous, as drovers herding their stock would stop at resting places – one, conveniently placed, 1.5 miles west of Calne, at Black Dog Hill. The Harris family saw the opportunity to make use of this ready supply and to expand their facilities so that pigs could stay locally for slaughtering and processing.

During the period of the Irish Potato Famine, 1845–49, the supply of pigs from Ireland started to decline. Thomas, Charles and George Harris saw their businesses seriously threatened and had to consider other ways of sourcing pigs.

In 1847, George, the youngest and most adventurous son of John and Mary Harris, left for America to explore the possibility of killing and curing pigs there and to ship back to England to sell. He left Portsmouth on 20 April and arrived in New York on 30 May, after a long, rough voyage: 'Many were the rolls, bumps, thumps and frights we received,' he wrote in his logbook.

He travelled all over the country by rail, riverboats and stagecoaches, stopping at Baltimore where he first saw bacon cured in an icehouse. He inspected ironworks in Pittsburgh, travelled 455 miles up the Ohio River to Cincinnati to visit the largest bacon curing establishment he had seen, and saw lard rendered by steam. He saw slaves in the south, working in the fields of Kentucky, and travelled to Montreal to visit US government workshops making guns and machinery. After a brief visit home, he returned, accompanied

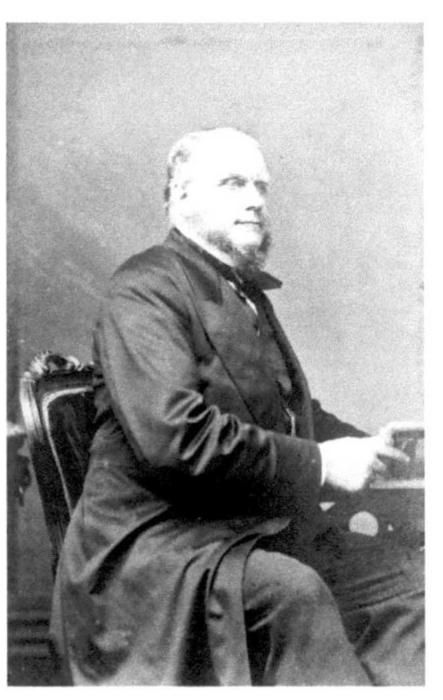

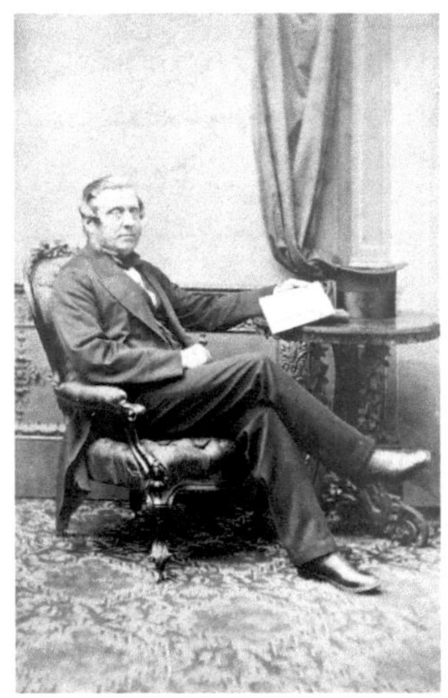

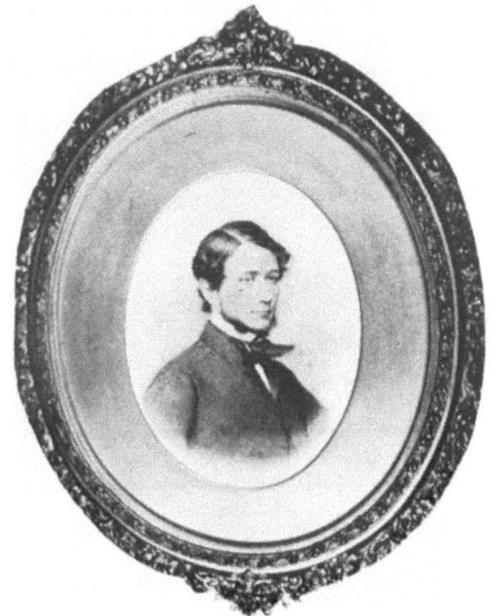

Above left: Thomas Harris, 1816–1908.

Above middle: Charles Harris, 1818–71.

Above right: George Harris, 1824–89.

by Charles, to set up a bacon curing company in Schenectady, New York State. It was not successful and the American Harris branch closed; the brothers returned home.

In spite of the failure of the enterprise, George's time in America had been very valuable. He brought back innovative ideas about cooling processes he had observed. This was to revolutionise meat processing, and completely change the fortunes of the family firm.

In 1856, an experimental icehouse was built at the back of the High Street shop. It had a thatched roof, a well-built false ceiling for storing tons of ice above the curing rooms, and cavity walls round the ice chamber filled with charcoal. They had tried sawdust but found that it heated up the building. The brothers employed people from the workhouse in the winter months to collect ice from local ponds and streams. During mild winters, ice was brought in from Norway on barges up the Wilts & Berks Canal. Now they could cure bacon all year round; best of all, they could lower levels of salt, previously needed for its preservation. A sweeter, milder cure became the favourite, and their reputation increased with its success.

The *Devizes Advertiser* reported in January 1869:

No ice having been found in sufficient quantity locally, we hear that our great bacon curers have entered into contracts for the delivery of a large quantity of ice from more northern climes, it being some years since such a delivery has taken place in Calne. This is a matter for regret, as it not only deprives the people of work of collecting the ice in a dull period of the year, but also puts the importers to a very considerable enlarged outlay.

After the death of Henry Harris in 1861, Charles and George formed a partnership in Butcher Row, while Thomas continued with the High Street business. The arrival of the Calne Railway in 1863 made it easier for Harris's goods to move around the country, which motivated further expansion.

In 1864, Thomas patented George's icehouse: 'An improved method of Constructing Rooms or Places for Curing and Preserving Meat or other Perishable Articles.' The income from licensing the patent to other bacon curers enabled the brothers to develop and modernise their premises.

After George's death in 1869, the business was left to his partner, brother Charles, who then became partners with Thomas. They kept their individual shops until amalgamation.

Over the next few years, Thomas expanded his High Street premises with a new icehouse and other buildings. A report in the *Devizes and Wiltshire Gazette,* 18 November 1869, was headed 'Reward for Hard Work':

Mr Thomas Harris has lately made great additions to his already extensive premises – new styes, slaughter-house, cellars, and a singeing furnace, have recently been erected. To commemorate this event and also to celebrate his fiftieth birthday, Mr Harris, on Monday evening took the chair at a substantial supper which he gave to his clerks, workmen and their wives, and also the artisans and labourers who had been engaged on the building. The festival was held in the new slaughter-house, a lofty and capacious hall of noble proportions, in the company of 170 persons, including many of Mr Harris's relatives and friends. The supper consisted of tea and coffee, joints of roast and boiled beef, and hams, followed by plum puddings and dessert. [The Harris family were teetotallers]

Charles Harris's reward to himself that year was to buy a 1790s former cloth factory, demolish it and build a Renaissance-style mansion, which he named Woodlands, set in its own small park, on an area between New Road and Station Road. Sadly, Charles died in 1871, aged fifty-four, but his family continued to live there until it became the home of Managing Director John Bodinnar, later knighted for his work for the government during the Second World War. After 1926, the premises served as offices for the company and for social events for Harris staff, and was extended in 1949.

Further refrigeration developments followed, with the patent taken out by Thomas Greenwood and Thomas Redman, George's nephew, announced in the *London Gazette* of 5 April 1878:

A new and improved method of constructing refrigerating chambers or chill rooms in combination with an ice chamber for cooling and preserving meat or other perishable articles of food by the use of natural currents of air, and for the improvement of the sanitary condition of airing rooms adapted to bacon curing and other provision trades.

Norwegian Ice Company advert, Kelly's Directory, 1898.

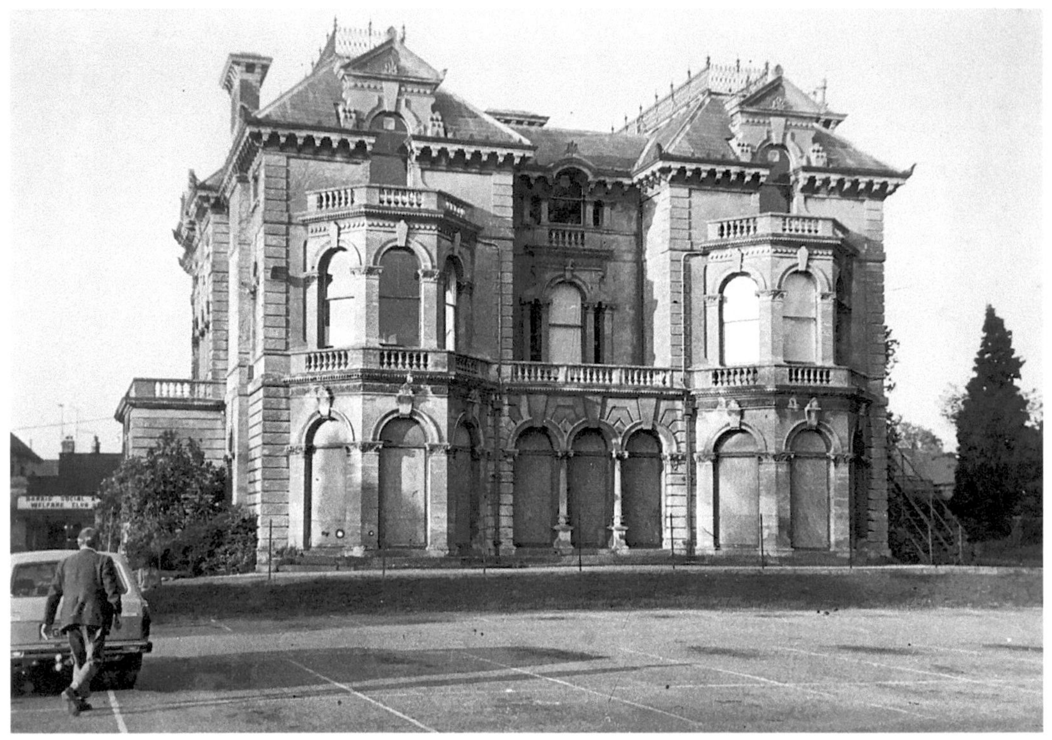

Woodlands, boarded up prior to demolition in 1983, was built *c.* 1865 for Charles Harris, in 'eclectic Renaissance style'. On the left, a sign for the entrance to Harris Social & Welfare Club is just visible.

Until 1888, Charles and Thomas ran their own businesses as two separate enterprises – Church Street dividing the factories. There was quite a bit of rivalry, according to John Bromham, especially in the labour market. 'An inducement of 1*s*-0*d* per week was sufficient for a man to cross the road from Mr Tom's to Mr Charles's, or vice versa.'

This period saw the beginnings of mechanisation of the production line. It was said that 'at the Church Street factory the pigs were moved almost entirely by machinery after they had been killed'. It was reported that on a single day just before Christmas in 1878, 'Messrs. Harris made a mile and a half in length of sausages'. Their reputation was further boosted when they took first prize and gold medal at the Royal Agricultural Society's International Show in London in 1880.

While the nation lauded Harris's success, Calne residents were admonishing them for the unpleasant after-effects of their business. There were many complaints over the years; one example, to the Local Board of Health in May 1883, was about 'abominable smells arising from the drains from a great deal of garbage which has been released into the sewers from the premises of Mr Thomas Harris, and other sausage and black-pudding makers.' Mr R. Henly reported that the stench was so bad in Quarr Barton that 'one could nearly see it'. It was resolved by installing stack pipes, in a suitable position near the Church Street buildings, which carried away obnoxious smells.

Another nuisance 'offensive and injurious to health' was reported, in November 1888: the dumping of refuse manure and animal matter in Northfields. The complainant wrote,

> I have repeatedly called the Messrs Harris & Co.'s attention to it and they readily gave orders to have the same covered up with earth; but where this is done, they immediately commence another heap in some other locality and so the nuisance is repeated, causing the most dreadful smell imaginable.

Factory expansion and modernisation continued. In 1885, the first mechanised refrigeration plant was installed: one 6-ton and one 4-ton Pontifex & Wood absorption machines in each of the two factories. Jesse Bullock was the first mechanic employed at Harris, and keenly embraced the new technology, heralding a new era.

Thomas, who was anxious to retire from active business life, agreed to a proposal by his nephew Herbert Harris to amalgamate the two firms under the two brothers' names.

Anyone with a spare £50 (equivalent to £6,541 today) could have done worse than invest in the newly formed company of Charles and Thomas Harris & Co., which was announced in the press on 6 September 1888.

> Among the joint stock companies recently registered at Somerset House is that of Charles and Thomas Harris and Co., of Calne, with a capital of £300,000 [£39,250,000 today], divided into 6,000 shares of £50 each. Object, the preparing, cure and sale of bacon, and other meat produce, whether derived from hogs or other animals, and the manufacture and sale of such other articles of food as the company from time to time shall deem expedient; the manufacture and sale of and other dealings concerning patent and other packages, tin and other cases, and canisters, wood and other boxes (whether lined or otherwise), bottles, jars and other appliances, containing or not containing any; of the materials manufactured or prepared by the company; the purchase of hogs and other animals, and also the acquirement of such appliances, ice and other articles used in the curing of bacon, as the company may deem expedient.

The purpose and practices of the House of Harris were set out clearly, showing how 118 years of growth had grown Sarah Harris's acorn into a giant oak.

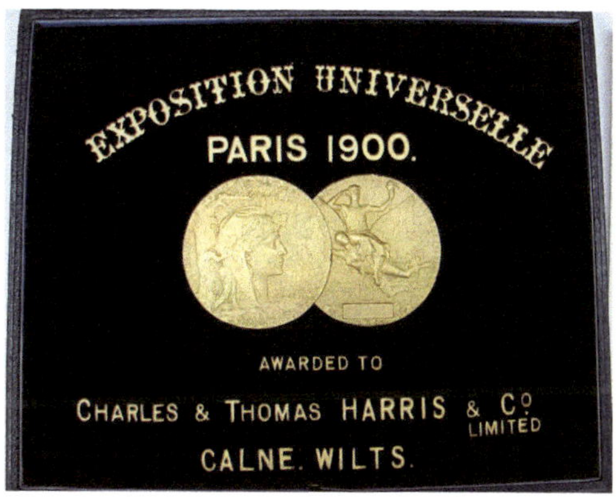

Gold medals were awarded at the 1900 Paris *Expositions Universelles*. Charles & Thomas Harris Co. were the only bacon curers who have ever received a first prize or gold medal at any International Exhibition.

The first subscribers included seven members of the Harris family, who were all entitled to be directors. This reinforced the family as the foundation and force behind the new company. In addition, John M. Harris, Tom Harris, Henry George Harris and Thomas Redman were appointed first managers of the company. The two premises were locally distinguished as No. 1 and No. 2 Firms.

In *The British Journal of Commerce*, January 1889, Calne was described as 'the chief seat of the bacon-curing industry of England'. Harris was exporting goods across the world, even producing special cures for meat going to hot climates.

In 1889 and 1900, Charles & Thomas Harris Co. were awarded gold medals for their exhibits of bacon, hams and lard at the Paris *Expositions Universelles*, the only bacon curers who have ever received a first prize or gold medal at any International Exhibition.

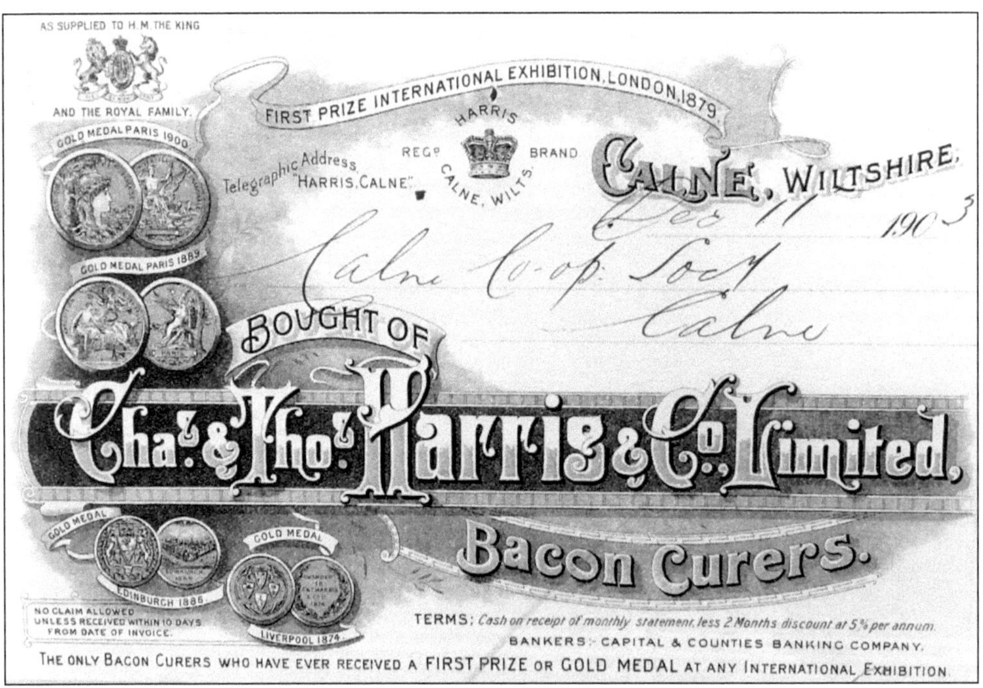

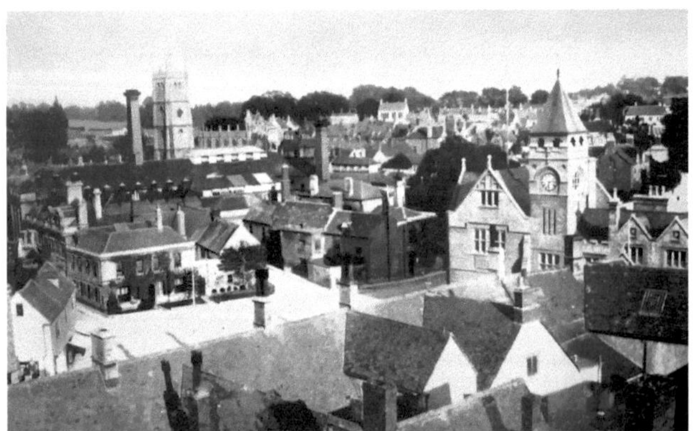

Above: Invoice from Chas. & Thos. Harris & Co. Ltd, displaying their many awards and prizes, 1903.

Left: 1896 view across The Strand to the Harris factory and St Mary's Church. The original Bank House (left), built in 1842, was used by the North Wilts Banking Co. They were taken over by the Capital and Counties Bank Ltd in 1878.

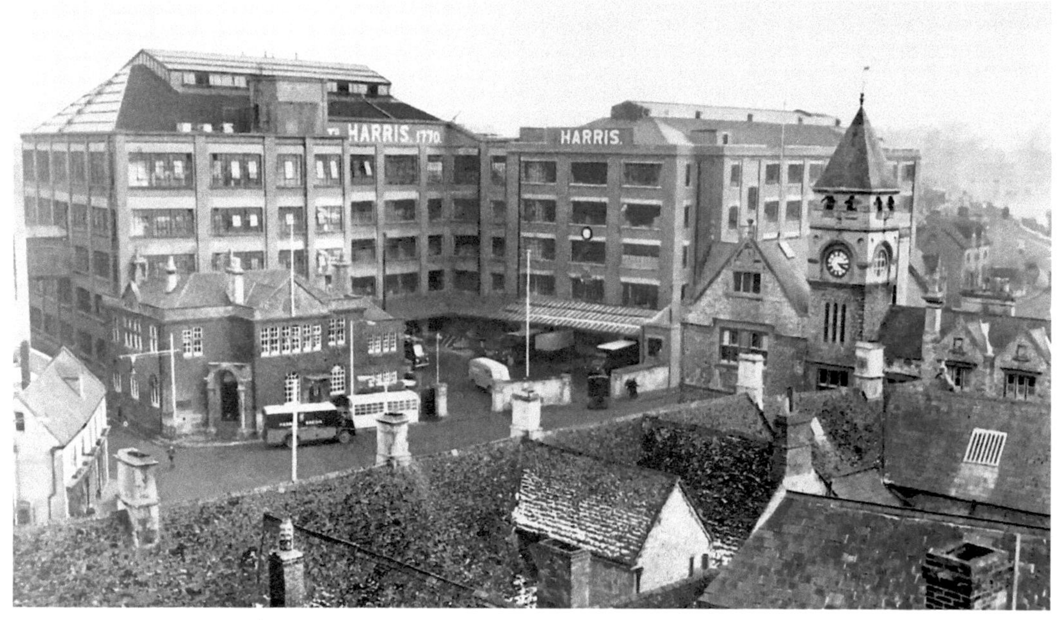

The same view in 1956, with Harris dominating the town centre. Old Bank House was rebuilt in 1900, and the premises were shared with Harris's laboratory and offices.

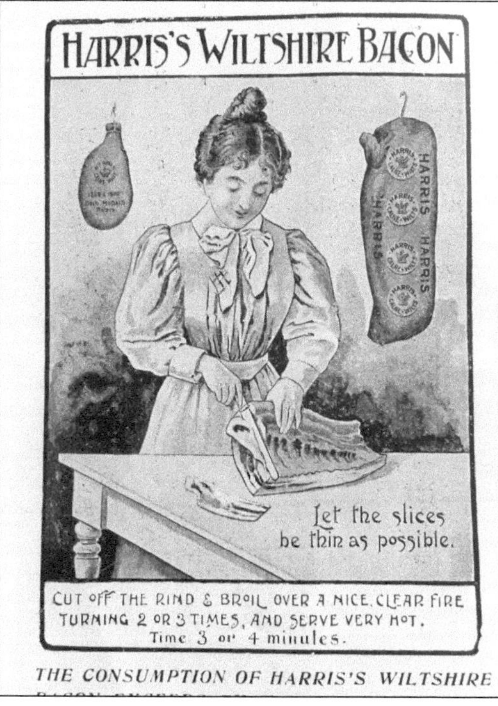

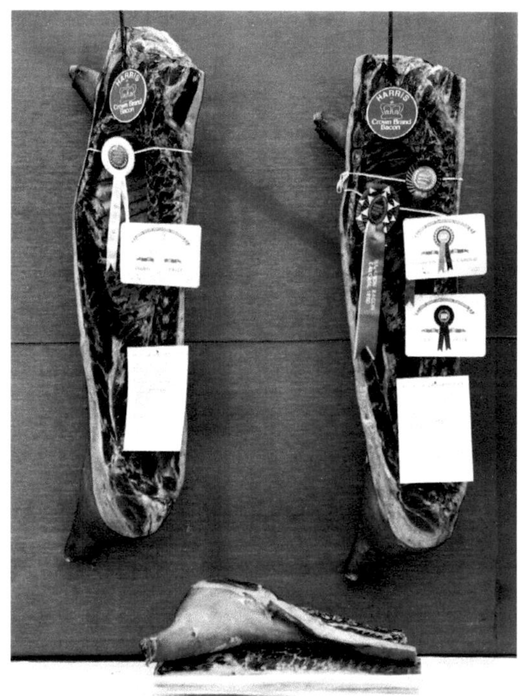

Above left: Harris's Wiltshire Bacon advert, *c.* 1900.

Above right: Sides of Champion Harris Crown Bacon, first amd third prizes, 1980.

2

The Building of C. & T. Harris, 1900–61

'The Firm have always been pioneers.'

Later retitled C. & T. Harris (Calne) Ltd, the company by now was world famous and held in high regard by all levels of society, including royalty; even across the Atlantic at the White House. The directors' minutes for December 1908 recorded an order for 'Sliced Bacon in tins, as well as other bacon to be shipped to Mombasa for President Roosevelt on the occasion of his forthcoming shooting expedition into Central Africa.'

Sadly, Thomas Harris was unable to appreciate this accolade. He died the same month in 1908, aged ninety-two. He had given his life to the family business, also serving five terms as Mayor of Calne. His funeral was reported in the *Wiltshire Times and Trowbridge Advertiser* on 12 December 1908: 'The town on Friday afternoon was given over to a respectful quiet and silence. Business was entirely suspended, every shop, public house and political club, being closed, and every window, on the route taken by the cortege had drawn blinds.'

The merger of the two Harris businesses led to a new period of growth, with the first major building programme when the two shop operations were moved to separate factories. The north-east of Church Street was largely assigned to pig slaughtering and bacon curing, while the south-west accommodated the expanding trade in small goods – sausages, lard, pies and cooked meats. New premises were designed to accommodate new technology and developments in meat processing.

In 1914, electricity was supplied by a 220-volt DC dynamo driven by a Lentz engine. In 1918/19, a new power station was erected in a central position between the river and Church Street. It housed four Lancashire boilers to supply the power station and the processing parts of the factory with steam. These are a type of horizontal stationary fire tube boiler invented in 1844 by Sir William Fairbairn. A Howden 400 kw triple expansion reciprocating engine was installed – the kind that was commonly found in large ships or in factories. The first landmark Harris's chimney was built 100 feet high and had an internal diameter of 5 feet 6 inches.

By 1925, Harris's own company provided electricity to the town, administered by the local council who combined it with their own gas service. By the 1950s the demand for power had grown and greater capacity was seen to be needed despite the fact that in 1954, the electrical supply for the town was transferred to the Central Electricity Generating Board. Harris continued to supply steam heating to the Town Hall and council offices, at least into the 1960s.

In 1920, local builders Blackford & Son, who had built Harris's curing cellars, slaughterhouses and piggeries a few years' earlier, were involved in a number of public works including widening the bed of the River Marden to prevent flooding at the back of Church Street, which happened periodically.

The flood, which still occurred that year, affected the construction work of No. 1 Factory, New Road, known as St Dunstan. This was purported to be the site of the assembly of the *Witenagemot* – the parliament of wise advisors, in AD 978, when the floor of the meeting house collapsed, killing St Dunstan's opponents, whilst he and his followers survived the catastrophe.

After 1920, the Harris family had little to do with the company, except George Henry, who occasionally visited the office to sign cheques. In 1922, the Marsh family of the Midlands-based Marsh & Baxter Ltd, famous for their York Hams, acquired some of the shares, which eventually led to a takeover in 1925 of 'the property and goodwill of all the home-produced bacon factories as going concerns'.

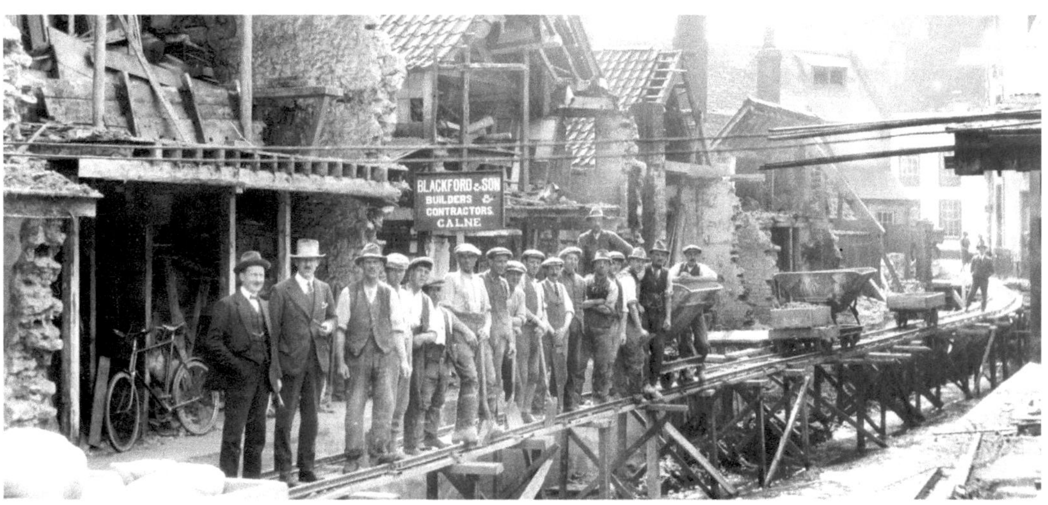

Blackford & Son working on widening the River Marden. It used to flood all the way up through Church Street. First, on the left, is James Herbert Blackford (junior) with bow tie and dark hat, son of the founder, 1920.

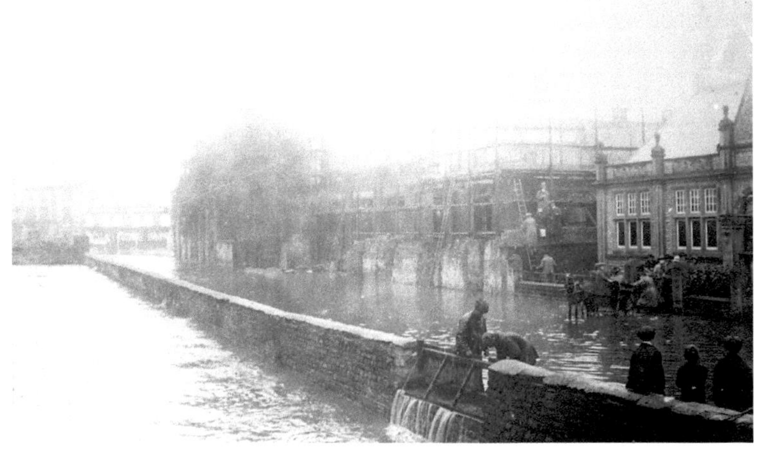

Calne flood, 16 April 1920. Children watch as women are evacuated from the library. Builders had to stop work on the new Harris factory as pieces of timber and building material were washed away.

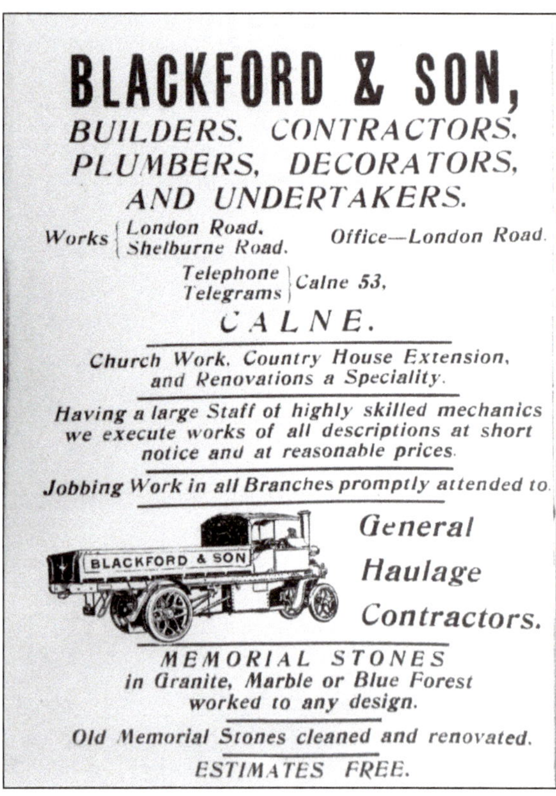

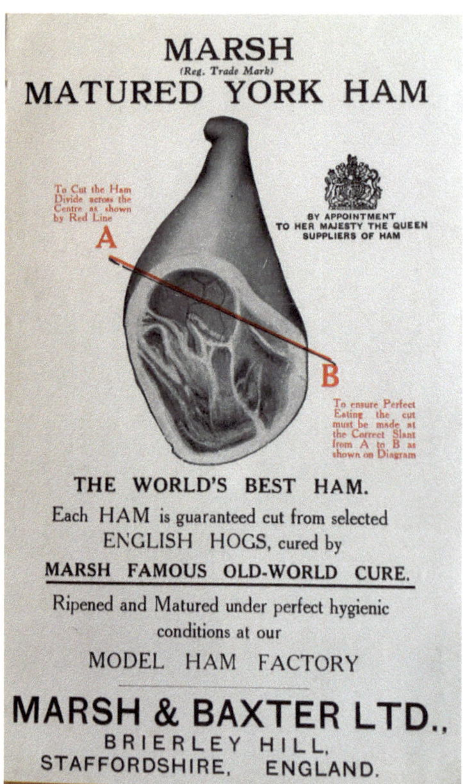

Above left: Blackford & Son advert, 1927. The business was started by James Herbert Blackford in 1884. The present-day family firm, Wessington Cabins, was registered in 1967 to 'manufacture, sell and hire portable toilets, cabins, showers, kiosks, containers and specialty units'.

Above right: Marsh York Ham advert. Marsh & Baxter Ltd was founded by Alfred Marsh, who bought a pork butcher's shop in High Street, Brierley Hill, Staffordshire, in 1867. They took over C. & T. Harris in 1925, keeping the Harris name.

With bacon curing still running in the Harris veins, John Mitchel Harris and his son, Raymond John Harris (son and grandson of Thomas Harris), acquired the control of Bowyer, Philpott & Payne Ltd, Trowbridge, in 1924. They changed the name of the company to Bowyers (Wiltshire Bacon) Ltd, and by 1957, the business was curing 1,000 pigs a week. It eventually closed in 2007.

At the beginning of the twentieth century Harris changed from a dry to a wet cure. This enabled the production of even less salty bacon with a much quicker turnover because the process took less time. This method was pioneered in the Danish Bacon industry; Harris's management recognised that this was the future.

The carcase was left to soak in a matured brine solution for three or four days and then drained off. The microorganisms in the mature brine transformed the nitrate in the mixture to nitrite, which sped up the curing. In 1937, large glazed tanks were installed in the factory to hold hundreds of carcases. Harris continued to produce fine quality dry cure but it was this wet cure that upheld their reputation in the twentieth century.

A new era began with the appointment of former Price Waterhouse auditor, John Bodinnar, as Managing Director in 1920, He was later knighted in 1941 for his service to the Ministry of Food (unpaid). He worked for Harris until his death in 1958. He brought growth and prosperity, overseeing expansion of the company, modernisation of the industry and improved working conditions for employees – setting up the institution of a works council, pension scheme and a bonus efficiency payments scheme. All kinds of social and recreational activities were established for staff and families across all the branches: sports clubs, amateur dramatics, reading groups, flower and vegetable shows, carnivals, children's parties, day trips and many more. He was made Honorary Freeman of the Borough of Calne in 1953 in recognition of his service to the town.

In 1926, Ernest Marsh set about modernising all the factories which Marsh & Baxter now owned. He appointed American architect, civil, structural and mechanical engineer, Dixon E. Washington, from Kansas City, who was seconded to the company. 'One of the last general engineers. He seemed capable of completing most jobs without the use of consultants or specialists – so prevalent today,' wrote John Bromham.

It is thanks to John (Jack) Bromham, who wrote *Memoirs of a Small Town Man* and *Brief History* of *C. and T. Harris (Calne) Ltd.*, that we have details of building work, machinery and production lines. He was born in Calne in 1909 and started at Harris as an apprentice

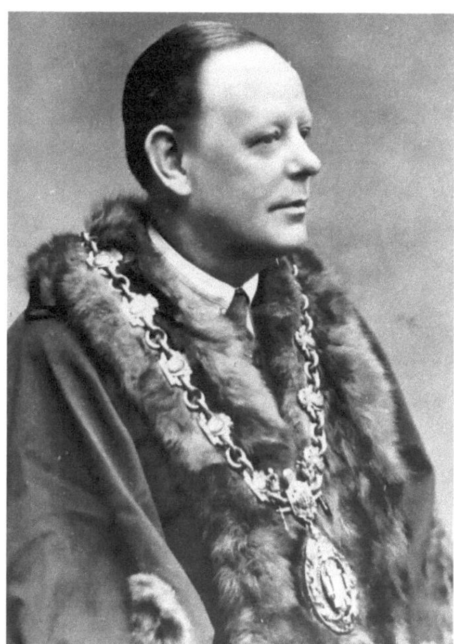
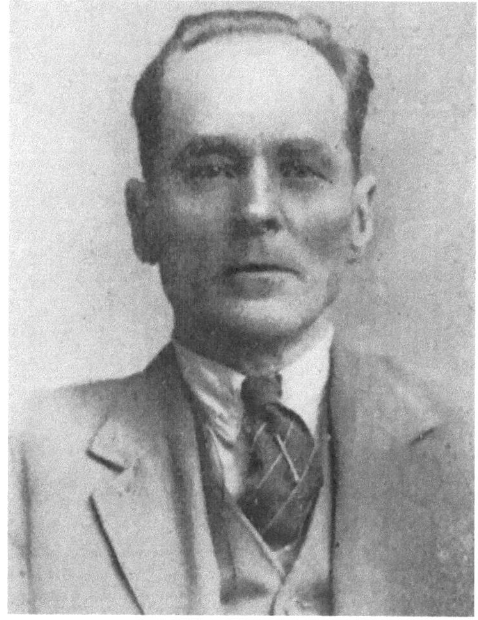

Above left: John Bodinnar, Mayor of Calne in 1925/26/27. He was knighted in 1941 for services to the Ministry of Food, 1941–45, and awarded Honorary Freeman of the Borough of Calne in 1953. Former President of the Food and Drink Federation, a room was named after him at their London HQ.

Above right: Dixon E. Washington, architect, civil, structural and mechanical engineer seconded from Kansas City, USA, by Ernest Marsh, in 1926 to modernise all the factories that Marsh & Baxter owned.

in 'general engineering' in 1926, on 10s a week. Seven years later, as a full craftsman, he was earning £3 5s.

At twenty-one, he became a draughtsman to Jesse Bullock, Chief Engineer, and was transferred to work with Washington on building the new factory. He rose to Chief Engineer, taking over from Jeff Edwarde in 1961/2. Bromham worked for Harris for fifty-four years, passing away in 2000.

The next phase of work, 1930–32, was collectively called No. 2 Factory, Church Street side. During the expansion of the premises, Blackford & Son were employed to carry out waterworks directed by Washington. From their account of the Harris work in *A Half-century and More of Building* (1934):

> This included Engine and Pump House and seven miles of nine-inch Mannesman Steel main, with a 750,000-gallon reinforced concrete reservoir. The ground [in the Woodlands] was excavated until a firm foundation was reached, then the reservoir was built clear of any vertical support, and covered with a concrete top. The pipe line was tested, with a 60 ft head of water, and not a single leak was found in the seven-mile length of pipe.

After about two years, it became apparent that the water was very corrosive and was no longer used.

The four-storey factory with basement was built with Cattybrook bricks, rich red bricks made by the Bristol company, which had supplied 74,400,000 bricks for the Severn Tunnel, which opened 1886; and Fry's Factory in Keynsham, built in 1920s. Bromham described the new factory: 'Steel-framed, with a Georgian-wired glass roof on a single span. On the lower floor, columns were at 20 feet centre. Each storey was 12 feet high.'

A rather romanticised account of construction work, 'Demolition, Excavation, Reconstruction' appeared in the *Harris Magazine* in March 1931:

> The impressive spectacle of men carving their way down into the crust of the Earth under the glare of powerful lamps, was witnessed with rapt attention by those onlookers in Church Street who watched the grey figures moiling and toiling down in the far greyer clay during the early autumn. To the imaginative workmen there must be something fascinating about incising, slicing and lifting up the earth's crust for removal elsewhere...
>
> Buildings of handsome and impressive design are arising, blessed with an ingress for sun and light and air, as the fit habitation of commerce and industry.

Further factory work continued in 1933–34. The existing power station was augmented by the installation of a Stirling water tube boiler providing steam to a new Bellis & Morcom steam turbine, which drove a Bruce Peebles generator. Coal came from the Midlands or South Wales for the boiler, which seems to have burned around 20 to 25 tons of coal a day, depending upon the demand for power. Some was delivered direct to the boiler house, but a stockpile was kept at Wenhill between the by-products plant and the Cattle Market.

Dry-cure and tank-cure cellars were installed, additional chill rooms and a hanging room were built, and new bacon-smoking stoves were added. A new office block was also built by Blackford & Son; some individual offices were lined with Japanese oak.

Between 1930 and 1956, Harris's bacon-curing capacity trebled. From 1940 onwards, Harris was ready to produce thousands of tons of food for the Armed Forces.

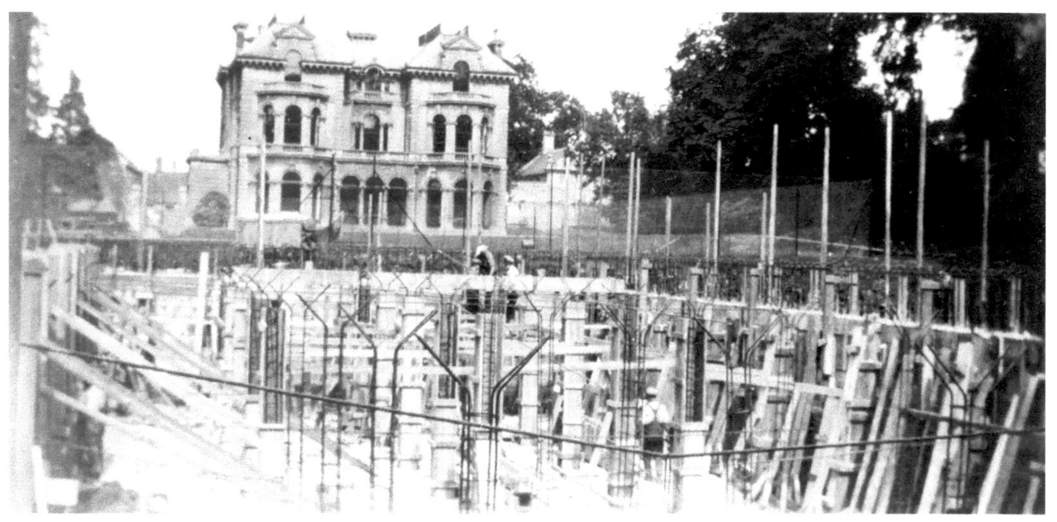

750,000-gallon concrete reservoir under construction by Blackford & Son at the Woodlands to provide water to the factory, *c.* 1930.

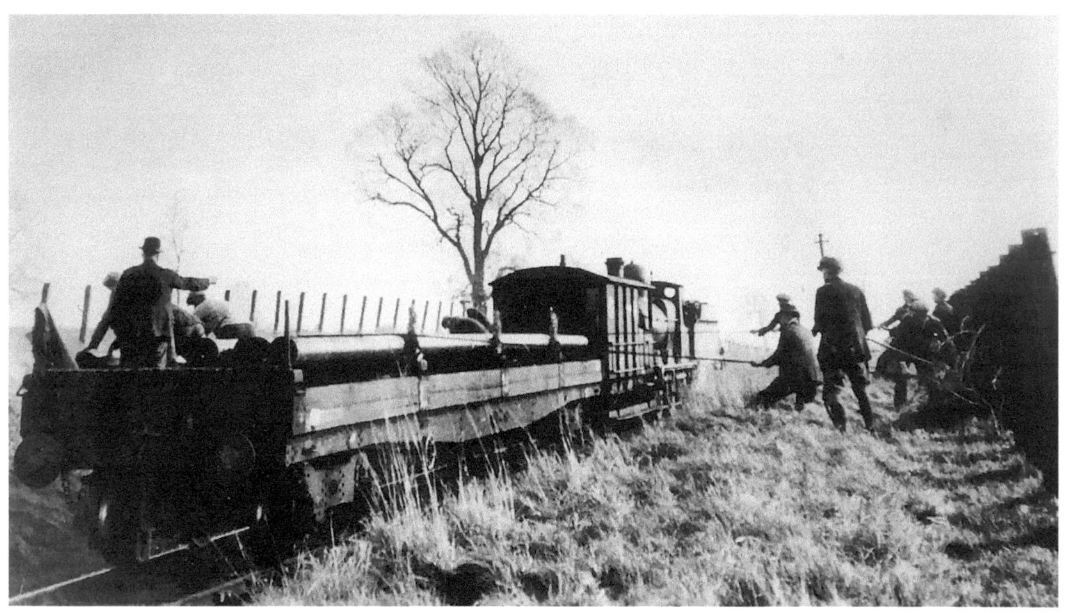

The Harris's pipe laying train, Blackford & Son, 1932. The pipes were laid alongside the branch line, bringing water to the factory from Langley Burrell.

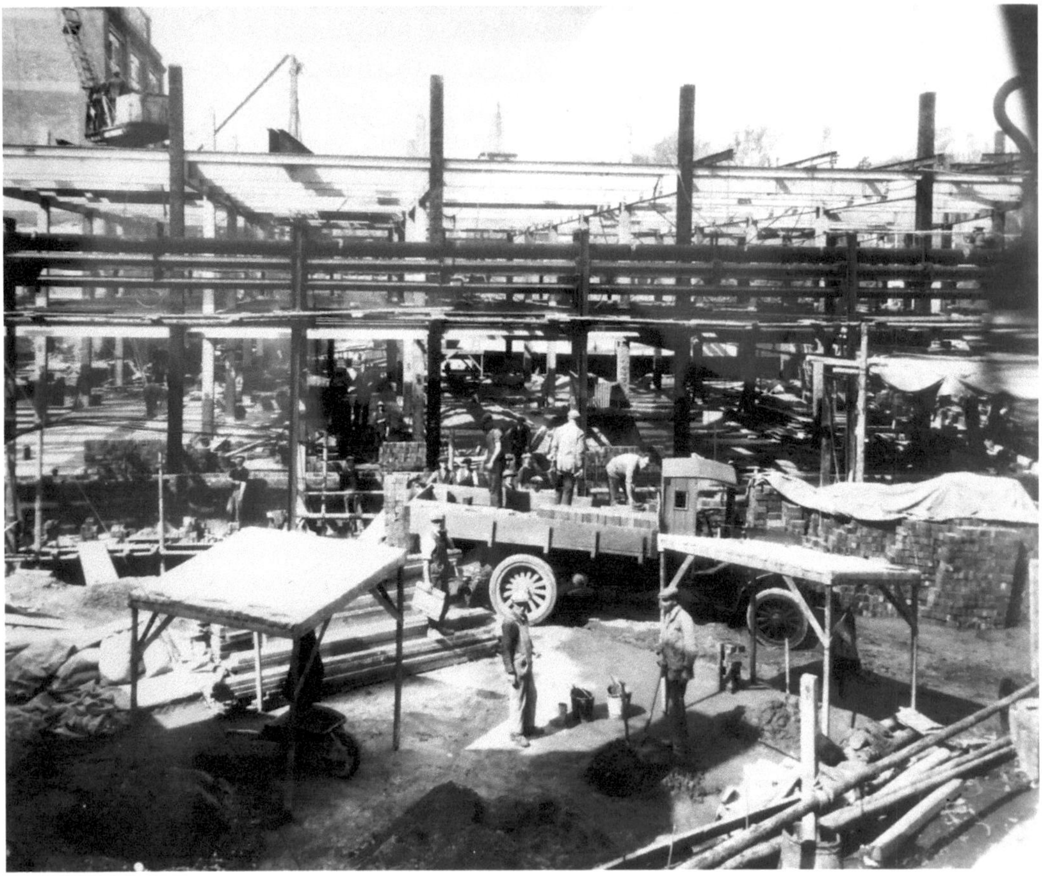

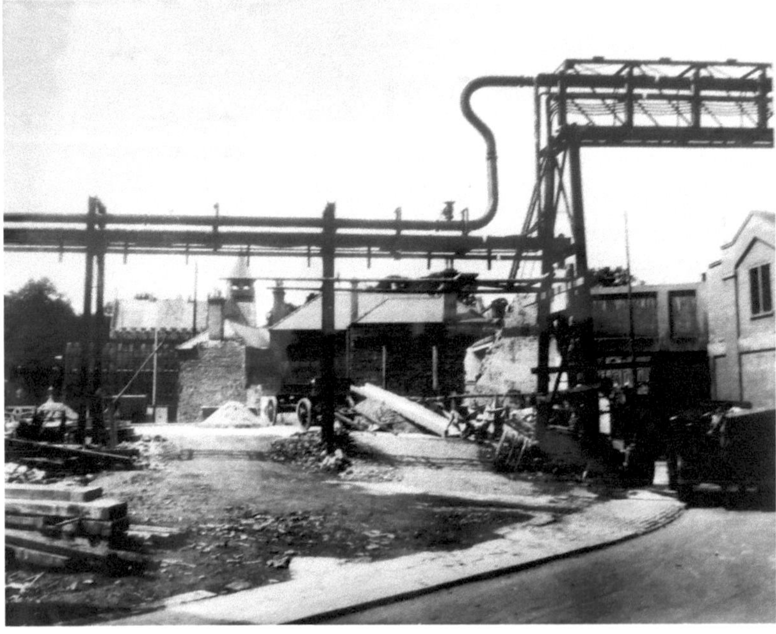

Above: View from Church Street of the construction of No. 2 Factory, 1930.

Left: View of No. 2 Factory site from Church Street with skeleton of the bridge for carrying service pipes and cables, 1930.

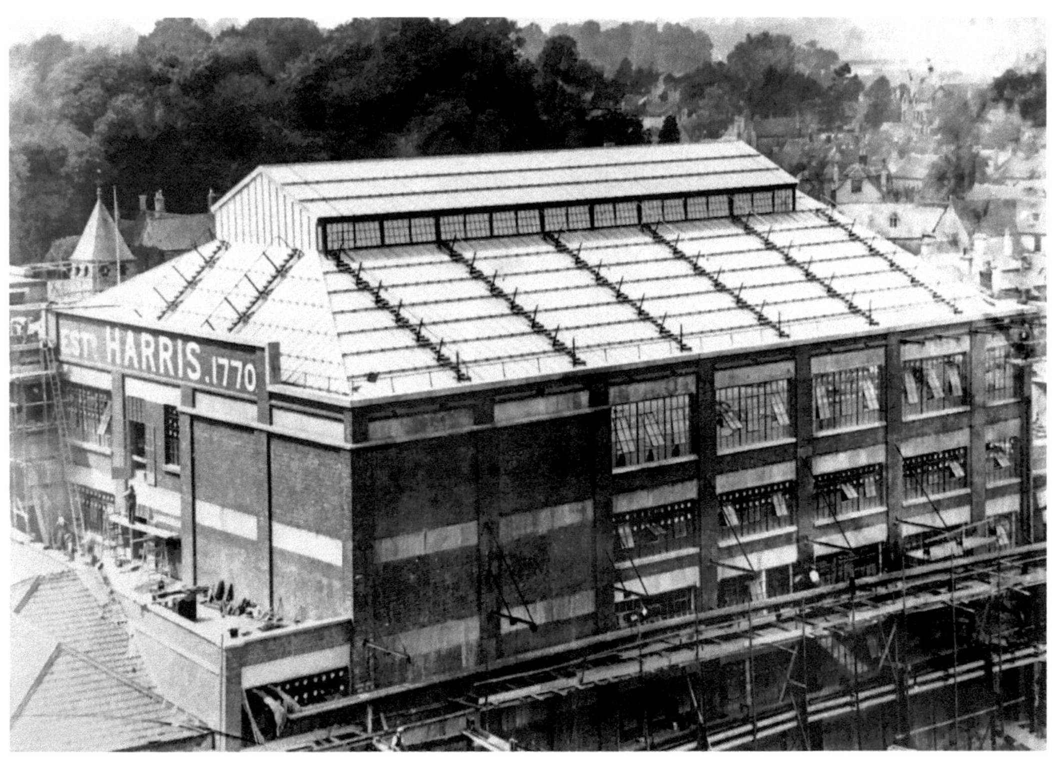

Roof structure, No. 2 Factory, 1931/2. 'Steel framed with Georgian wired glass roof on a single span' provided plenty of light for workers.

Calne Factory Extension.

SOME INTERESTING FIGURES.

The building stands on an area of 18,000 square feet, and consists of six floors of an average height of 12ft., each floor being level with the existing floors of St. Dunstan's Factory.

	TONS.
The estimated weight of building is	10,500
The footings are designed to carry an additional	12,300
Total weight of concrete footings is	2,200
The largest footing is 42ft. long, 8ft. 6in. wide, and 6ft. 10in. deep, containing $1\frac{1}{4}$ miles of reinforcing steel and weighs ...	163
The total quantity of reinforcing steel is	130

If placed in one line would reach 81 miles.

Weight of concrete floors	4,000
Weight of structural steel	1,000

Weight of Portland cement on whole job 1,500 tons.

Amount of sheet cork used to insulate chill rooms, &c.—130,000 square feet.

Number of clinker bricks used on the floors—1,130,000.

By comparison the number of bricks required for the walls is small, being only one half-million.

A special feature is the fifth floor. There are no interior columns on this floor, thus giving a clear space rather larger than the existing Hangar Store at the station.

It will be covered with a totally glass roof, and well ventilated. The area of glass used in roof will be 18,600 square feet. Weight of steelwork used in roof—125 tons. Number of window panes required is 5,136, representing an area of 12,000 square feet. The total enclosed volume is 1,500,000 cubic feet.

D. E. WASHINGTON.

Dixon E. Washington, in charge of the 1930–32 factory extension, reported details of its construction in the *Harris Magazine*.

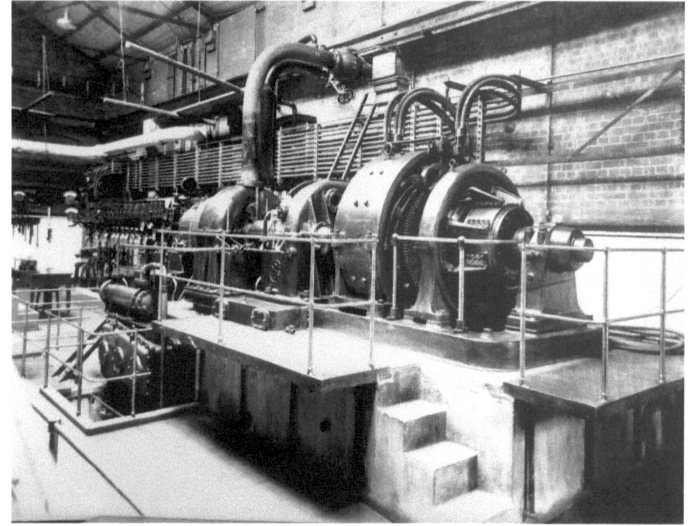

The old power station with 1934 Bruce-Peebles generator at front, connected to Bellis and Morcom steam turbine at the other end. In the background to the left, the main electrical switchboard for the factory can be seen.

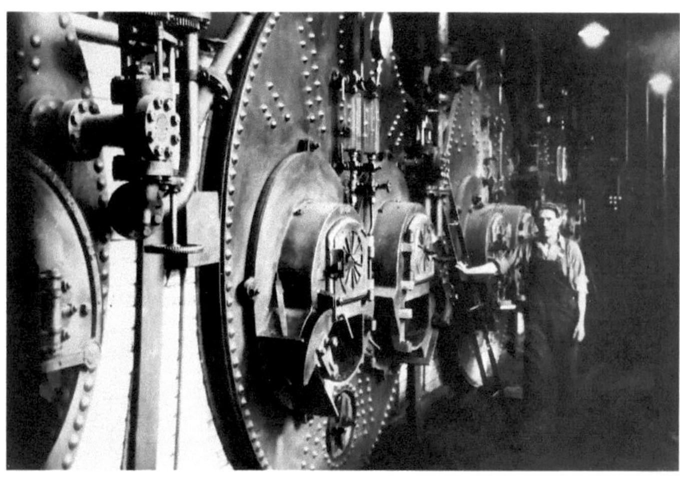

Jabez Dean in the front of Lancashire boilers in the Church Street boiler house, taken before the Second World War as after that, they were fitted with mechanical stokers.

As Commercial Secretary and Head of Supply Department, Ministry of Food, 1941–45, Bodinnar already had twenty years' experience of the food industry.

Harris supplied thousands of tons of rations to the troops, tinned meat being an important product. Canning and the sterilisation of meat had been introduced in 1918. Bottled goods such as brawn, tongues and pastes were still sold in glass jars and were gradually replaced by cans; Harris continued developing the process.

Directors' meeting minutes from July 1943:

> It was reported that the patent application for the Canned Skinless Sausage invention in joint names of the Company & Mr M. R. Redman in respect of a device for producing Canned Skinless Sausages & that the Ministry of Food were interested in this invention and had requested the Company to grant licence to their sausage manufacturers.

During the war, J. Sainsbury Ltd suffered badly during the London air raids, and eventually their pie-making operation was evacuated to Calne, along with some of their workers. Links between the two companies continued post-war, with an annual get-together, which included a cricket match and a feast.

In 1953, directors received an unexpected letter from George A. Hormel & Co., Austin, Minnesota, expressing interest in working with Harris to manufacture Hormel's famous meat product SPAM in the UK. First produced in 1937, SPAM became very popular during the war, especially to feed the troops. After months of research and financial estimates, the Board recorded their reasons for turning down the offer:

> We would need to allocate a complete floor of the factory to the product and to incur expenditure of approximately £50,000 [equivalent to £1,405,329 today] on the plant. Also required, the provision of new office accommodation. There would be an interference with the production lines and difficulties would arise over the use of parts of the carcases not required for SPAM production.

During 1954 to 1956, under the management of Chief Engineer Jeff Edwarde, former shops in Church Street were demolished for a large new boiler house, complete with an additional tall, red-brick factory chimney, opposite Bank House. Beside the boiler house but set back from the street, a new turbine hall was also constructed, into which were installed a further, but much bigger, Stirling type boiler and another Belliss & Morcom/Bruce-Peebles steam turbine and generator set, which was larger than the 1934 one. At the time, the new boiler was one of only two in the country.

The company continued to buy more land, properties and other businesses, expanding their empire with factories and warehouses across the UK, which together became The Harris Group. In 1957, C. & T. Harris, Calne, employed 2,116 workers.

Harris advert, 1934, announcing that their pigs are 'painlessly anaesthetised before slaughter by an electric device certified by leading scientists as the most perfect and humane method known'.

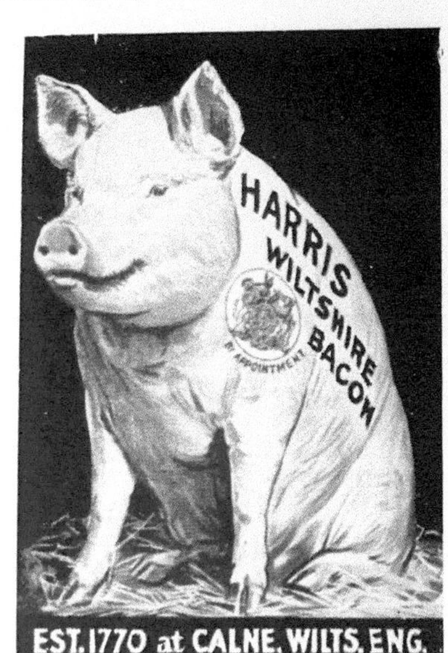

In 1960, Marks and Spencer (St Michael brand) became Harris's most important customer. They insisted on separate work areas, personal liveried delivery vehicles, and their orders took priority over others. M&S made regular inspections, many unannounced, which kept management and workers on their toes.

The Marsh family, sole owners of the Harris Group, remained in charge until the company takeover in 1962.

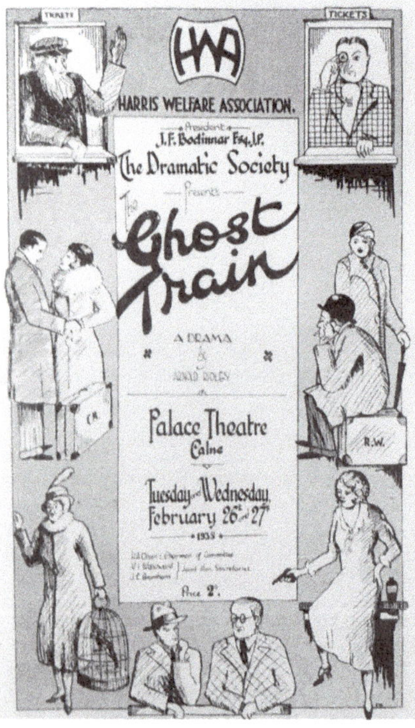

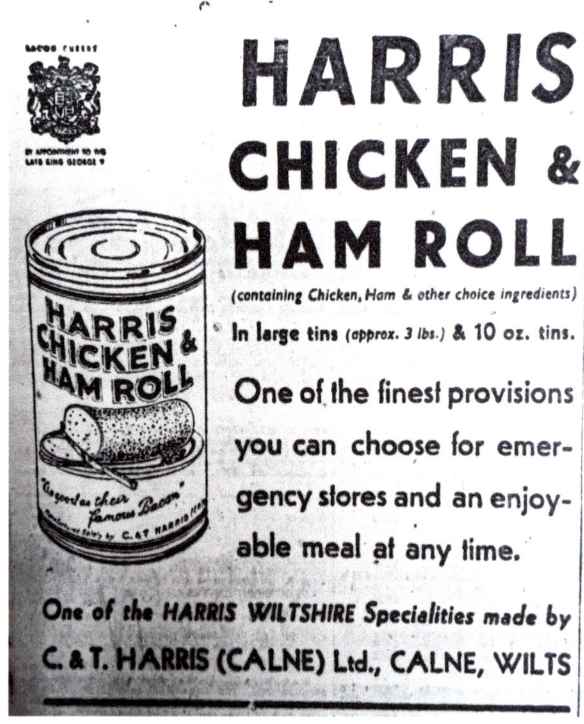

Above left: 1935 poster for the production of *Ghost Train* by Arnold Ridley (who played Private Godfrey in *Dad's Army*). John Bodinnar was president of Harris's Dramatic Society.

Above right: Advert for large 3 lbs and 10 oz tins of Harris Chicken and Ham Roll 'for emergency stores and an enjoyable meal at any time,' *Daily Mail*, 1939.

Left: Brawn recipe for the NAAFI, 1944. It was made mainly from parts of pigs' heads including eye pieces – eye muscles that attach eyeballs to bony eye sockets, said to be the tastiest meat on a pig.

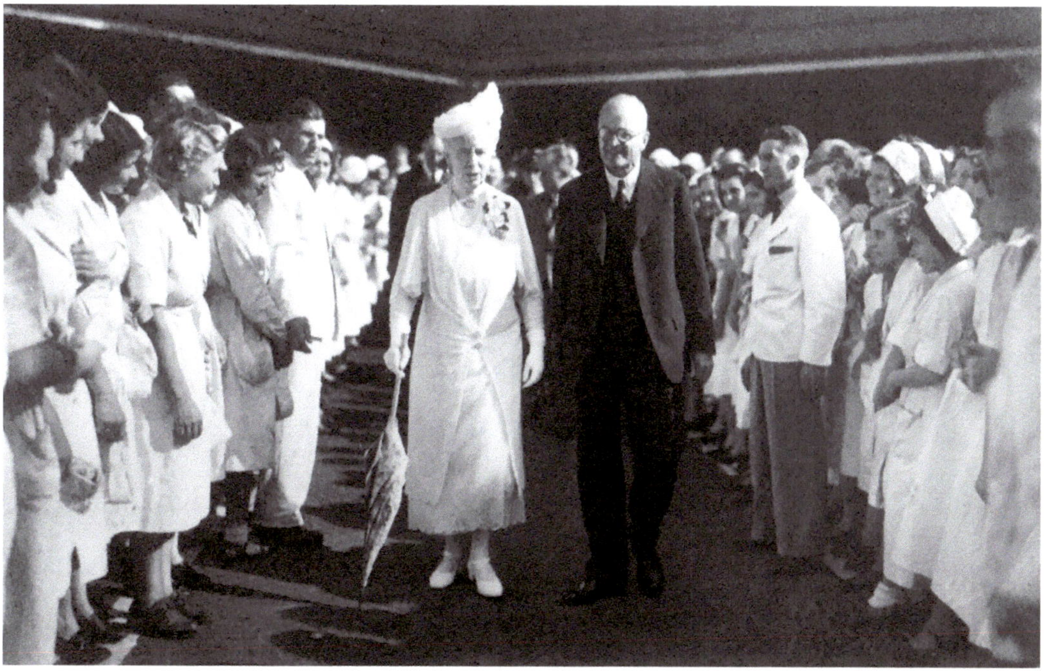

Above: Queen Mary visiting the Harris factory in 1941 as part of the war effort, accompanied by local director Percy Redman.

Right: Programme for C. & T. Harris Children's Xmas Carnival, Woodlands Club, 1953. (Marc Harding)

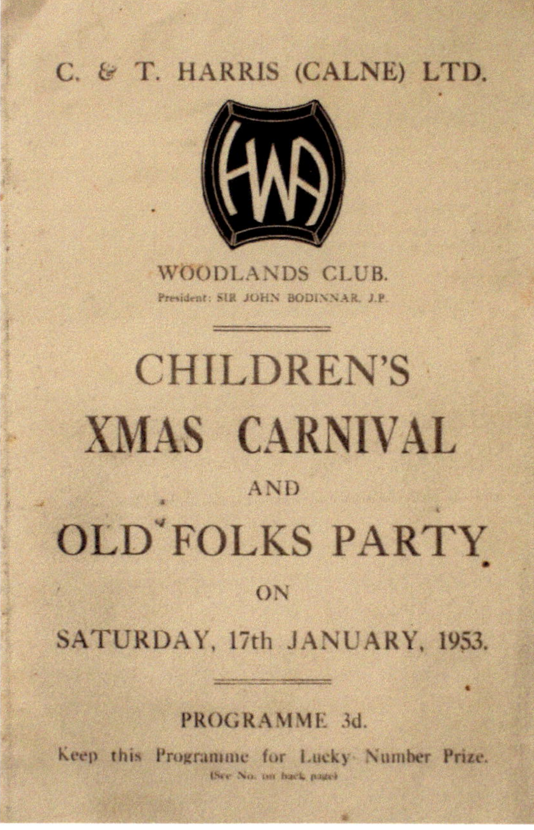

C. & T. HARRIS (CALNE) LTD.

WOODLANDS CLUB.
President: SIR JOHN BODINNAR, J.P.

CHILDREN'S
XMAS CARNIVAL
AND
OLD FOLKS PARTY
ON
SATURDAY, 17th JANUARY, 1953.

PROGRAMME 3d.
Keep this Programme for Lucky Number Prize.
(See No. on back page)

DETAILS OF SOME OF THE COMPANIES MAKING UP THE HARRIS GROUP

C. & T. HARRIS (CALNE) LTD.

Head Office and Main Factories at

CALNE, WILTS.

Branch Factories at
REDRUTH,
TOTNES,
TIVERTON and
KIDLINGTON (Oxon).

Warehouses at
LONDON,
BIRMINGHAM,
CARDIFF,
LEICESTER,
MANCHESTER,
LEEDS,
NEWCASTLE and
GLASGOW.

HARRIS (IPSWICH) LTD.
Factories at
IPSWICH and
NEEDHAM MARKET, Suffolk.

ROBERT SEAGER LTD.
Retail Shops at
IPSWICH.

HARRIS (EASTLEIGH) LTD.
Factory at
EASTLEIGH, Hants.

WILTSHIRE BACON CO. LTD.
Factory at
CHIPPENHAM, Wilts.

HIGHBRIDGE BACON CO. LTD.
Factory and Creamery at
HIGHBRIDGE, Somerset.

THE DUNMOW FLITCH BACON CO. LTD.
Factory at
DUNMOW, Essex.

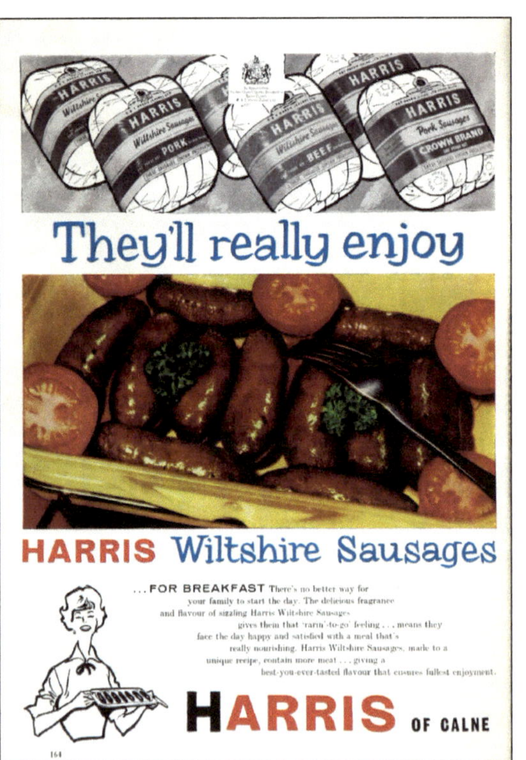

Above: List of companies in the Harris Group from Careers with the House of Harris, 1956.

Left: Harris advert, 1960. (*Grace's Guide*)

3

The FMC Years, 1962–82

'People, profit, and capital will make the expansion of FMC possible.'

Chairman D. H. Darbishire, 1979

The next phase of development began with the takeover by the Fatstock Marketing Corporation. Set up in 1954 by the National Farmers' Union (NFU) as a farmers' organisation for 'the grade and deadweight marketing of meat', it became a public company, FMC Ltd, in 1962. Headed by Chairman Sir John Stratton, it acquired the Marsh Harris Group in a deal worth £7 million (equivalent to £150,334,000 today). FMC was 'the largest producer-controlled organisation of its kind in Europe'; about 80 per cent of its shares were held by farmers.

It was a challenging time, with severe winters in 1962/3, swine disease in Holland and Belgium, and a declining pig population in France, which drastically reduced the number of pigs available in Europe. In addition, there was a shortage of imported beef, which caused a squeeze in profit margins and the collapse of negotiations with the Common Market, which might have been able to address the issue of pig supplies. It took two years to recover from these events.

In October 1966, Sir John Stratton was elected chairman of the British Bacon Curers' Federation and at a press conference said: 'The curing industry is in the midst of the biggest crisis in its history. Every pig cured means a net loss of 30 shillings (£1.50) or more of the present price of pigs and bacon.' In the December *FMC News*, Stratton said that the shortage of pigs has been directly responsible for the high prices, which had made bacon curing an uneconomic operation.

FMC newsletters reported on the industry, financial issues, investments in new technology and modernisation at branches, including Calne. From *This is Harris,* 1972:

Large new open-plan offices have recently been opened, including the FMC Group Computer Centre which is used extensively by C. & T. Harris. The boiler plant has been converted from solid fuel to North Sea Gas and the two tall chimneys, once a landmark, have been demolished. The opening of the section of the M4 motorway bypassing Calne has eased traffic problems in the town and greatly improved vehicle access to the factory. The Calne factory has its own printing plant producing price lists, stationery and promotional literature. There are excellent staff facilities and social club.

Throughout the history of pig breeding, the holy grail was the perfect pig. In 1962, Harris appointed its own geneticist, Mr J. L. Jollans, BA, St John's College, Cambridge, who lived and worked on a local farm and pig unit. In *This is FMC*, March 1976, pig rearing was a topic:

At FMC's Pig Development Unit, great progress has been made in improving food conversion and carcase quality by means of genetic selection. The unit comprises four farms: Marden Farm, the research centre; Wansdyke Farm, with a multiplication herd, Rough Leaze (Wiltshire) and Honeyclose (Yorkshire). Tested boars and gilts [females under the age of one-year] are in strong demand at home and overseas.

Harris maintained its reputation across the world. One company that had been dealing with Harris since the 1950s was the Pacific Agencies Co. Ltd in Hong Kong, a very large importer and exporter, providing supermarkets on the islands with their bacon, black puddings, liver sausage, pies and canned food. One of their directors, Mr John Mak, visited Calne, receiving a very warm welcome at the factory; customer loyalty was the mark of a successful business.

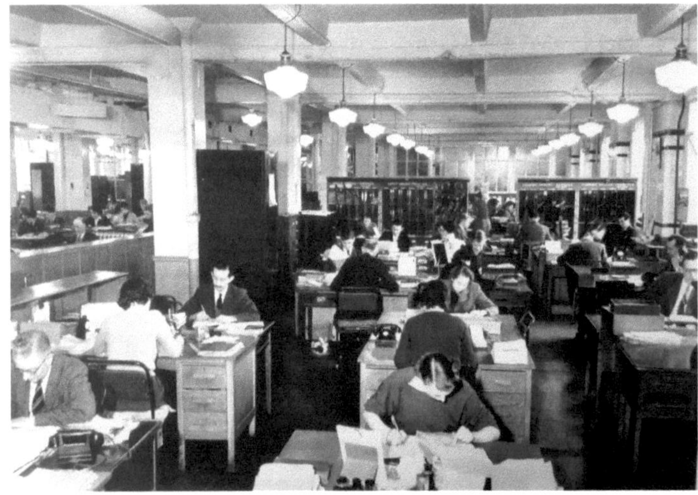

Sales and General Offices, 1950s.

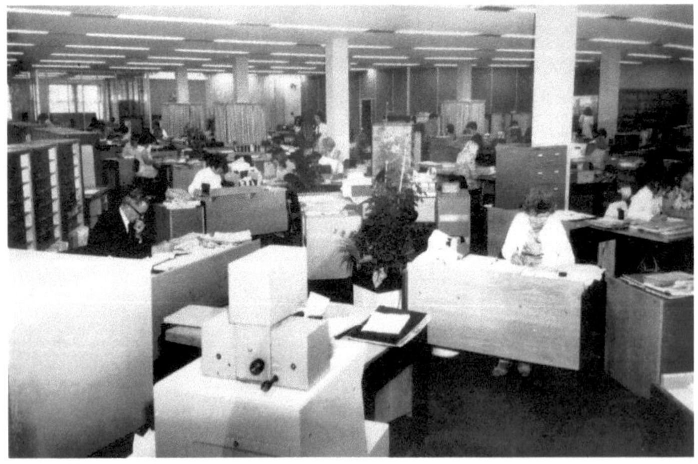

New landscaped offices at Calne, 1973. The 17,000 sq. ft floor area was laid out so there were no straight passages or line of desks. 'This avoids the bugbear of regimentation,' said Roy Beck, Secretary and Chief Accountant.

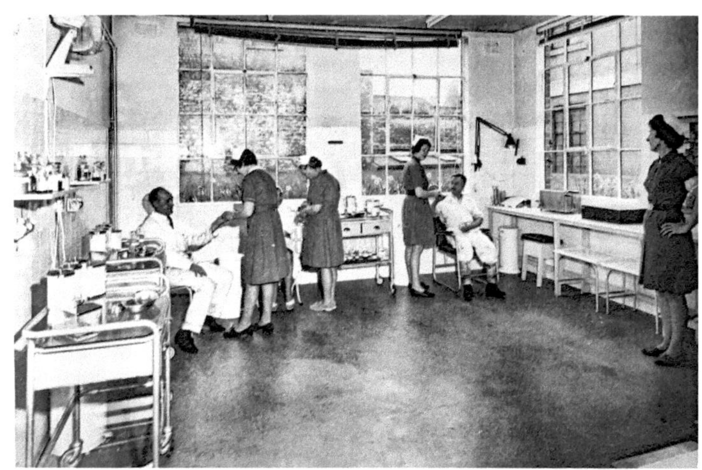

Harris Medical Room opened in April 1969, providing twenty-four-hour care for employees. Sister J. H. Arthur was in charge with Mrs A. Logan as state-enrolled nurse. FMC magazine, 1979.

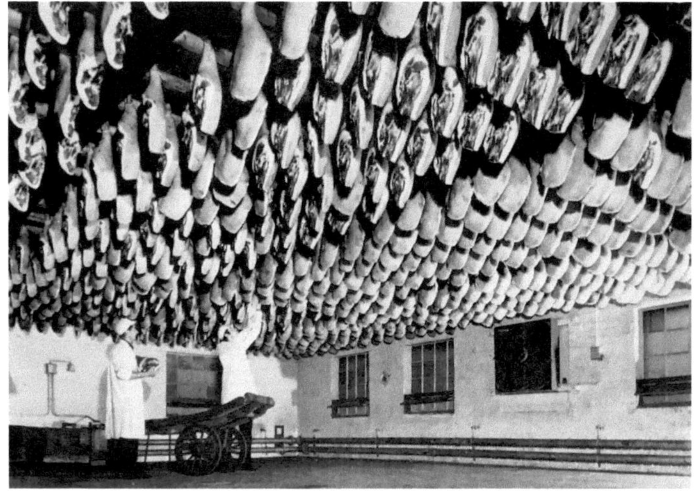

York Hams hanging in cellars, Marsh & Baxter's Brierley Hill factory, 1976.

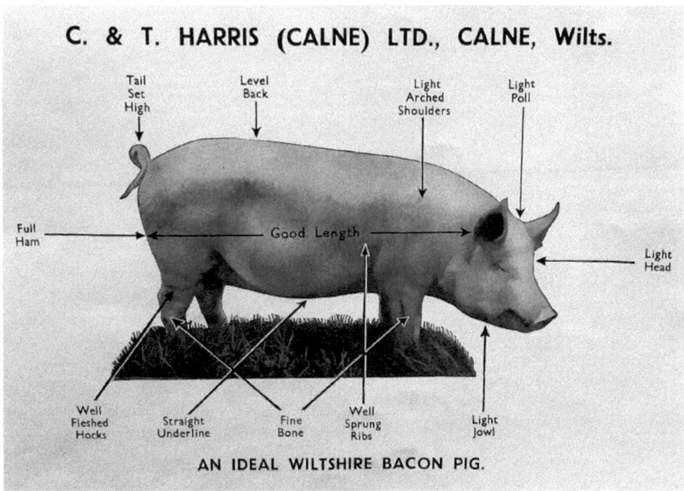

An Ideal Wiltshire Bacon Pig – the Large White Yorkshire. 'There should be no rolls of coarse fat at the jowl, or over the neck and no depression between the hams at the root of the tail. Hair, fine and silky.'

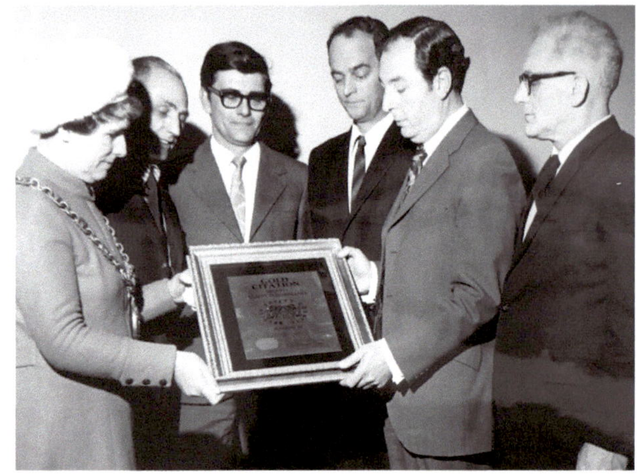

Presentation of British Safety Council Gold citation, 1974. The first time for Harris – one of only twenty companies that year. Mayor Cllr Ethel Hornby is holding the certificate with Chris Absolon, Group Manager (fourth from the left), and Dick Baggs, No. 1 Factory Manager.

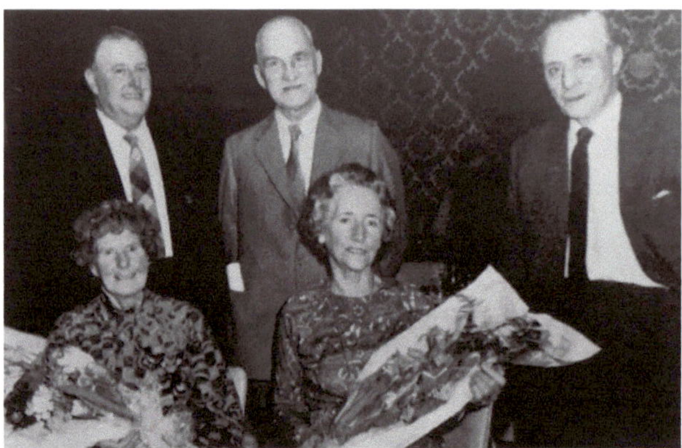

Retirement party, Woodlands Social Club, January 1974. Left to right: Jack Bromham, Chief Engineer; Bill Butler, Senior Clerk, Ledger Department; Joe Shrimpton, Head of the Wages Department – total 120 years' service. Front row, Mrs Frances Bromham and Mrs Shrimpton.

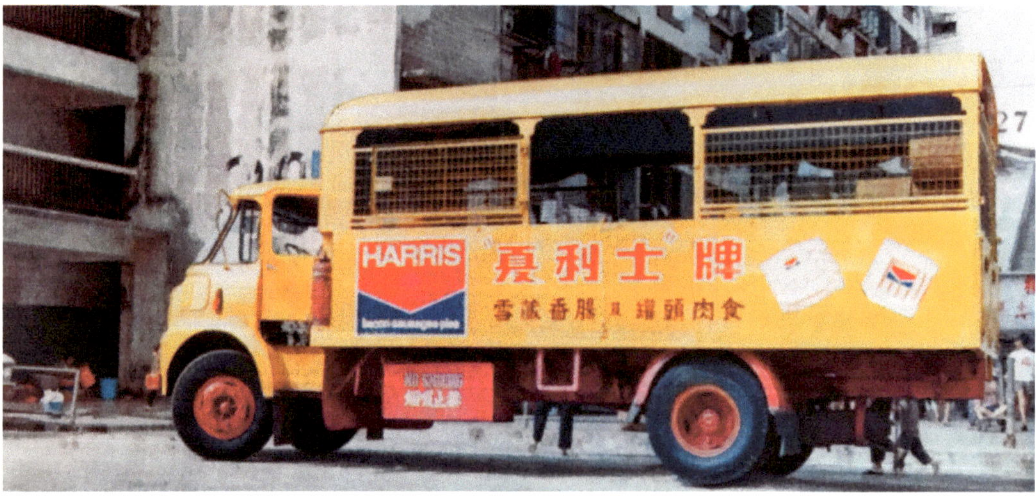

Austin van with threepenny bit cab (angled sliding doors) from Pacific Agencies Co. Ltd, Hong Kong, 1974. The company had been dealing with Harris for over twenty-five years, supplying supermarkets on the island with their sausages, pies and canned foods.

4

Transport

Canal, Rail and Road

From the early days of drovers travelling by foot to deliver pigs to market, to more recent times of goods trains and refrigerated lorries, C. & T. Harris was always looking for ways to improve and expand its distribution network.

The Wilts & Berks Canal was essential for the traffic of commodities such as ice, coal, sawdust and salt to the factory. The branch followed the right bank of the Marden, passed through a tunnel under the London–Bristol road, terminating at the Wharf in the town centre. An arch of the Stanley Aqueduct had collapsed in 1906, after breaches in 1901, and the canal formally closed in 1914.

The arrival of the railway in 1863 linked Calne to the main lines, changing the fortunes of the company yet again. The first Calne Railway Company (CRC) train arrived from Chippenham in 29 October 1863, loaded with 100 pigs and other goods, including coal. Pigs were driven on foot from the station up to the centre; escaping pigs in the streets became a common sight.

The new single-line track followed the left bank of the Marden. It was built on Brunel's broad gauge, which remained until 1874 when it was converted to standard gauge. Stanley Bridge Halt was built in 1905.

Charles, Thomas and George Harris, original directors, contributed more than half the money towards the CRC. The Great Western Railway worked the line but the local company continued to own it until its amalgamation with GWR in 1892. The total cost reported in the newspapers was £54,000 (equivalent to £6,830,000 today).

At the celebratory dinner held at The White Hart, Chairman of the Board Mr T. L. Henly, praised 'Five small individuals in a small place have made a small railway; but small as the railway was, it had not been a very small undertaking.'

Lord Lansdowne acquired a quarter of an acre of land at Black Dog, and in 1874 a siding off the main line was built for his private use – to unload coal and other heavy goods at the nearest point to his home, Bowood House. In spite of Black Dog Halt not being a public station, passengers would get on and off there. In 1952, it was officially recognised with a name board. Railwayman Douglas Lovelock was appointed stationmaster and lived in the private station for more than thirty years.

Calne Railway's days were numbered – as road transport increased and revenue from the line decreased. The whole track needed replacing, and Stanley Bridge Halt required repair work. It was recommended for closure in the 1963 Beeching Report.

It was sad to see the end of one of the best-known lines in the country, its reputation made during the Second World War. Due to Calne's proximity to the Radio Schools at

RAF Compton Bassett and Yatesbury, it conveyed large numbers of personnel to and from the camps, as well as tanks and equipment.

The first Calne stationmaster was Mr George Neate; the last one was Ewart Ponting, who had worked for the GWR from 1916 to 1965. The last train from Calne was on 18 September 1965.

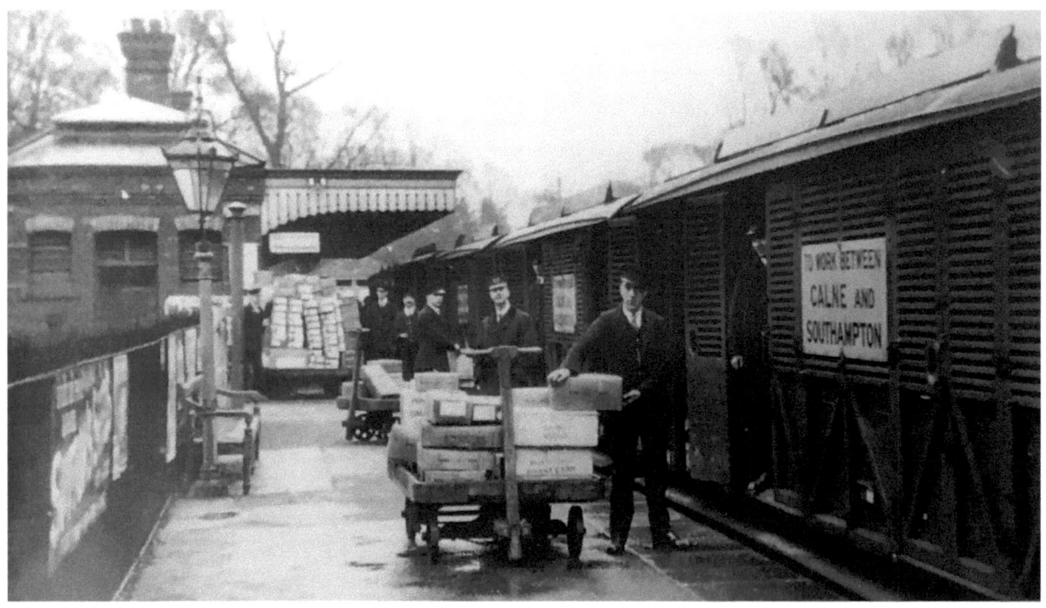

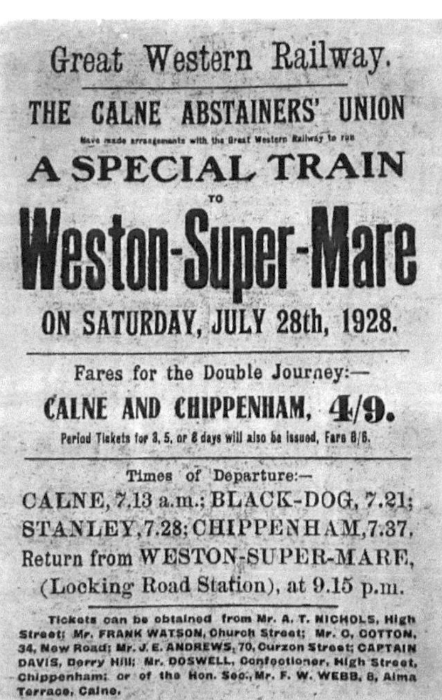

Great Western Railway.

THE CALNE ABSTAINERS' UNION

Have made arrangements with the Great Western Railway to run

A SPECIAL TRAIN

TO

Weston-Super-Mare

ON SATURDAY, JULY 28th, 1928.

Fares for the Double Journey:—

CALNE AND CHIPPENHAM, 4/9.

Period Tickets for 3, 5, or 8 days will also be issued, Fare 8/6.

Times of Departure:—
CALNE, 7.13 a.m.; BLACK-DOG, 7.21;
STANLEY, 7.28; CHIPPENHAM, 7.37,
Return from WESTON-SUPER-MARE,
(Locking Road Station), at 9.15 p.m.

Tickets can be obtained from Mr. A. T. NICHOLS, High Street; Mr. FRANK WATSON, Church Street; Mr. O. COTTON, 34, New Road; Mr. J. E. ANDREWS, 70, Curzon Street; CAPTAIN DAVIS, Derry Hill; Mr. DOSWELL, Confectioner, High Street, Chippenham; or of the Hon. Sec., Mr. F. W. WEBB, 8, Alma Terrace, Calne.

S. Carpenter, Printer, Calne.

Above: Calne station, *c.* 1925. In the foreground, boxes of 'Finest Lard' and sausages are being loaded onto Harris's branded vans.

Left: GWR poster for Calne Abstainers' Union summer trip, 1928. The Harris family were teetotallers. Thomas Harris was the President of the Western Temperance League and one of the founders of Calne Abstainers' Union.

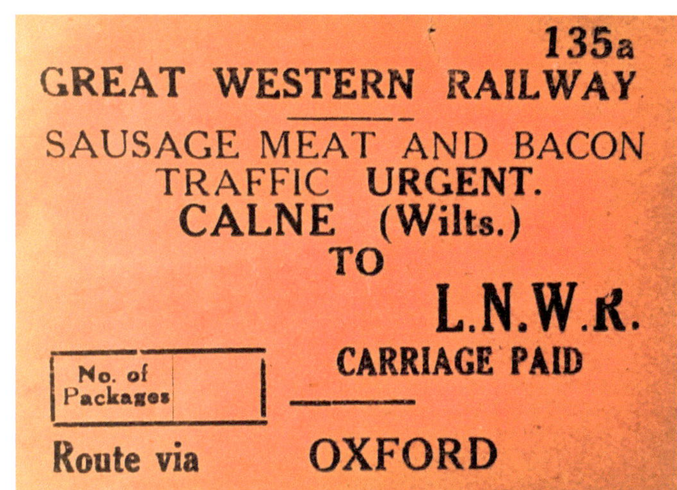

GWR identification slip for goods travelling by rail.

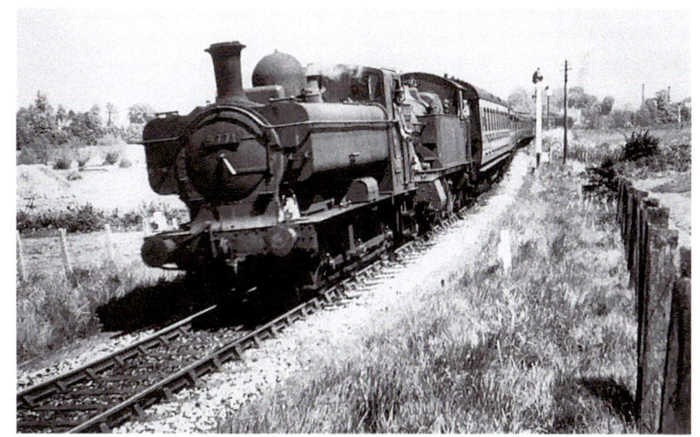

Calne branch train, 1950s.

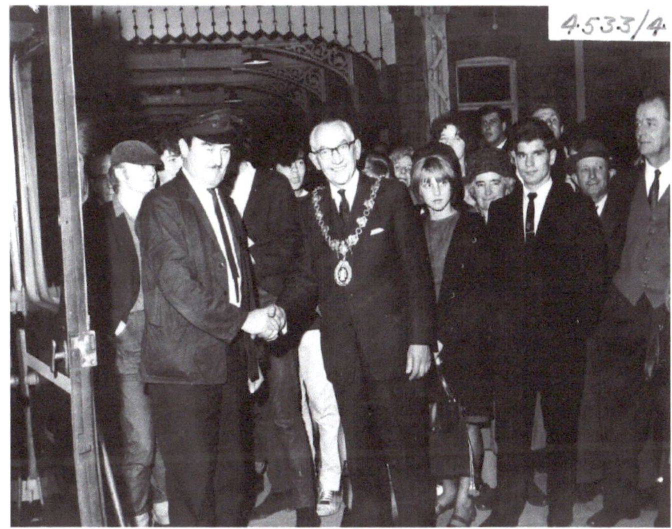

Farewell gathering for the last train from Calne, 19 September 1965. On board driver Frank Cannon (left), a railwayman of thirty years' service, Mayor Harold Walter Weston and Mayoress. Geoff Taylor, principal cornet player in Calne Silver Band, sounded 'The Last Post'.

Harris had long been investing in road transport for the distribution of goods to retail outlets across the country: steam lorries (wagons) and combustion engine vehicles. Directors' minutes from 1 November 1907:

Motor Lorry
The question of sending goods to the Midlands and South Western Railway junction at Marlborough by road, to compete with the Great Western Railway was considered, and as we had been offered a motor lorry by the Ryanfield Motor Co. Ltd it was decided to write to them saying we would accept their offer of a 5-ton rubber tyred lorry for a month's trial at a fee of £13 per week, inclusive of driver, fuel, insurance, tyres etc., subject to our purchasing same at the price of £750 [equivalent to £90,817 today].

Five van salesmen were first employed in London in 1920. By 1930, Harris had a fleet of forty-four vans all over England, Wales and Ireland. Each man was responsible for sales and distribution in a specific region.

It was announced in the *Western Daily Press*, 9 September 1931:

Messrs C. and T. Harris (Calne) Ltd, the enterprising Wiltshire firm, announced that they are commencing this week, daily deliveries, by their own motor vans throughout Bristol and district, of their famous Wiltshire sausages and ready-cooked table delicacies. This will be a very great convenience to grocers and provision merchants in the district, and will ensure that the public will be able to obtain readily, supplies of these much-desired commodities a few hours after their manufacture in the firm's model factory on the glorious Wiltshire Downs.

In 1956, there were over a dozen factories, eight warehouses and a fleet of 300 motor vehicles managed and controlled from offices in Calne. The Engineering Department was responsible for all the maintenance of vehicles, using its own workshops.

To someone like Traffic Manager James Smellie working for Harris (1935–67), the loss of the railway had a huge impact on the company, and on his own work. His daughter Barbara Sealy remembers how he would work all night with piles of papers on his desk at home, planning the logistics for the increase in road transport distribution.

After the FMC takeover, Blue Rosette (Transport) Ltd was formed in December 1965, and its headquarters moved in 1976 from Wembley to the Woodlands where the offices were. In 1969, according to *Mileage,* the Dunlop Company Ltd newsletter, FMC owned and maintained about 1,100 commercial vehicles, and looked after 400 cars used by company employees throughout the FMC Group. Their workshop was at Wenhill Heights, and paint shop in The Pippin.

FMC News, in 1979, reported the huge cost of transport: 'A new refrigerated sales van costs £10,000, and a large articulated trunker costs £50,000 [equivalent to £254,600 today] with each of its fourteen tyres costing £125 each [£636 today].'

Mike Bennett was Vehicle Inspector at the MOT Station at Porte Marsh Road from 1968 to 2008. He handled all types of vehicles from the area, including all of Harris's. 'They were always in excellent condition – very well looked after by Blue Rosette.' After retirement, he took his knowledge and expertise to the Atwell-Wilson Motor Museum, where he is one of the trustees of the charity.

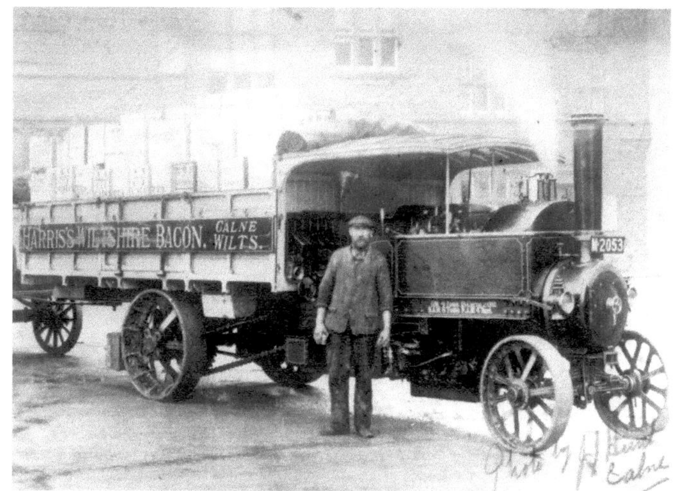

Foden 5-ton steam wagon No. 1679, supplied new to C. & T. Harris in 1908, in front of the Lansdowne Strand Hotel, loaded with crates of produce bound overseas to places such as Calcutta and New York. (Roger Onslow)

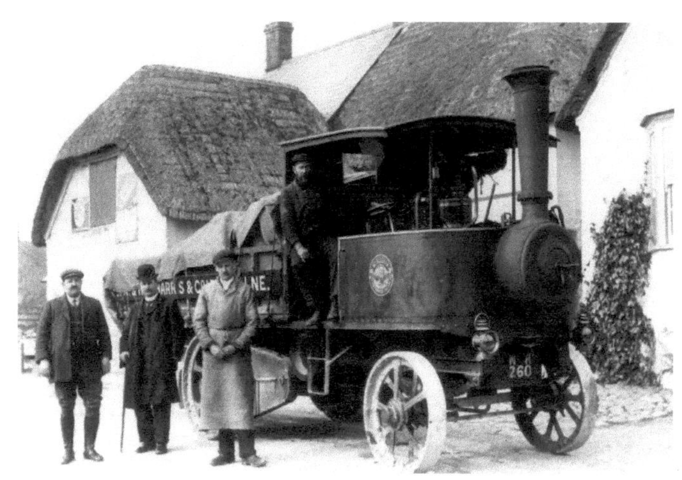

Allchin steam wagon No. 104, with Harris driver Richard Onslow, Waggon and Horses, Beckhampton, *c.* 1910. William Allchin (& Sons) Ltd, formerly Globe Works, Northampton. stopped building steam engines in 1925, having only built about 220 over the previous fifty years. (Roger Onslow)

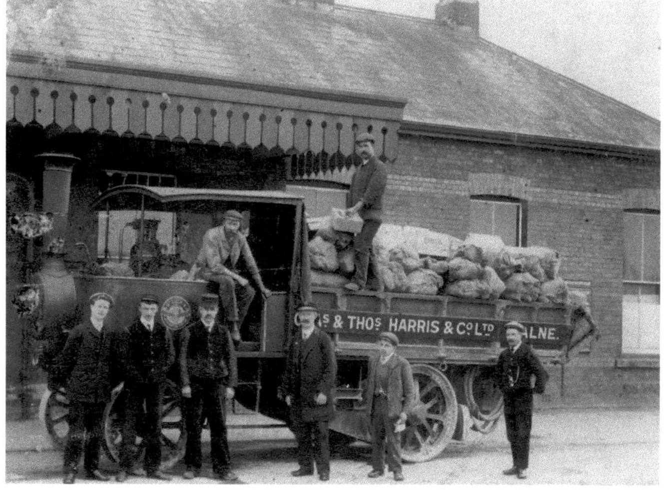

Harris Allchin steam wagon No. 104. Richard Onslow, driver, delivering Harris produce to Marlborough Station, *c.* 1910. (Roger Onslow)

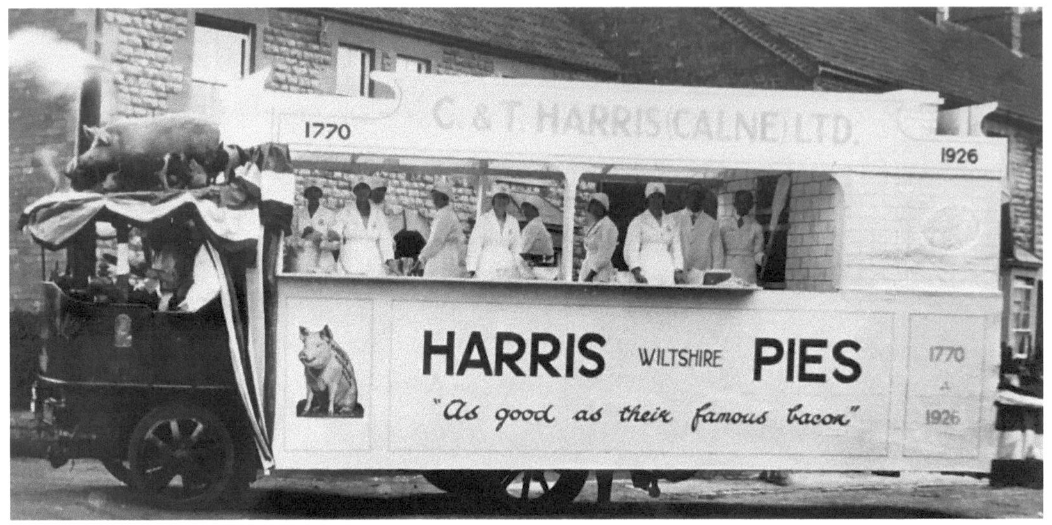

Harris's Sentinel steam lorry, advertising Calne Shopping Week, The Pippin, 1926. Staff would throw free pies to people passing by.

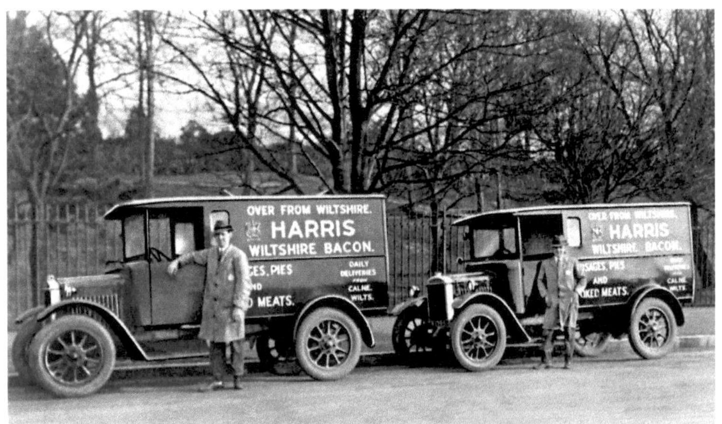

Over from Wiltshire, Belfast Morris vans with salesmen J. F. May and R. Miller, 1920s. Van salesmen started in London in 1920 with five men. By 1930, Harris's had forty-four vans across England, Wales and Northern Ireland.

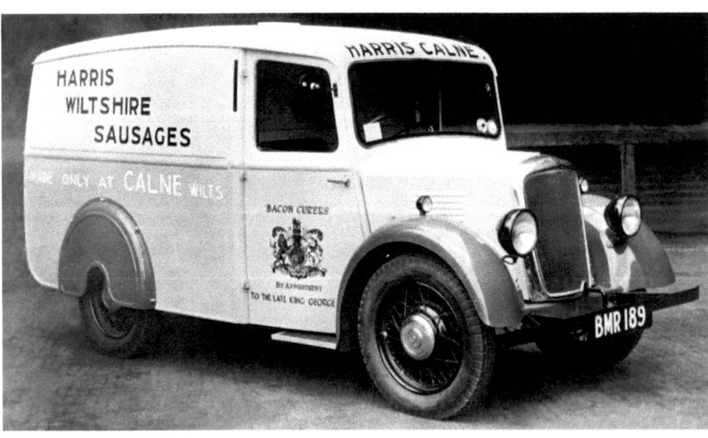

Two-tone Morris 10 cwt series 2 van, registration 1937/38.

Scammell Scarab three-wheeled tractor unit, aka mechanical horse. 'They were a common sight in Church Street and The Strand, scurrying to and from Calne station, taking Harris goods as well as fetching coal,' remembers Bob Bromham.

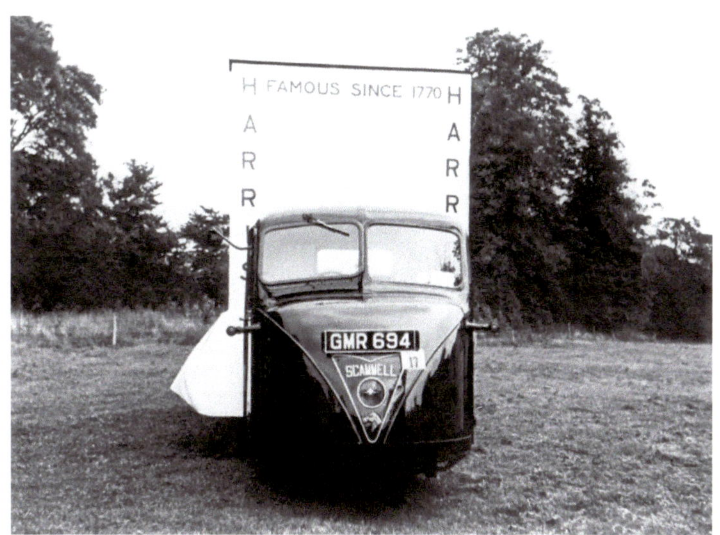

Two Leyland Octopus Harris Bacon lorries, 1960s.

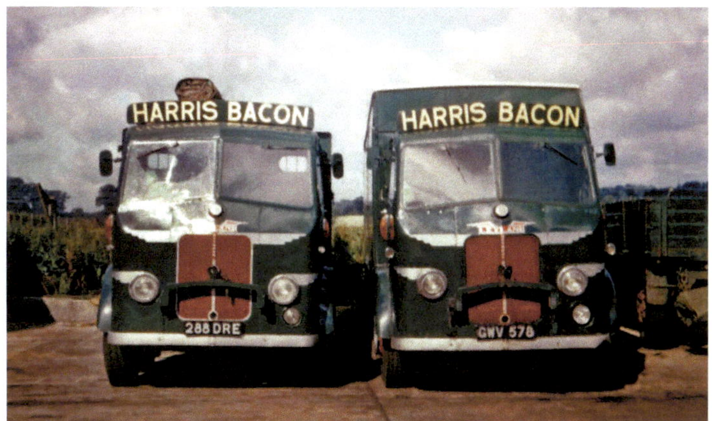

Left to right: Dick Baggs, No. 1 Factory manager; John Coltart, No. 2 Factory Manager; John Godwin, Traffic Manager; Frank Lovelock, Wiltshire Bacon Company Manager; with the first lorry of the new fleet of Leylands, 1965.

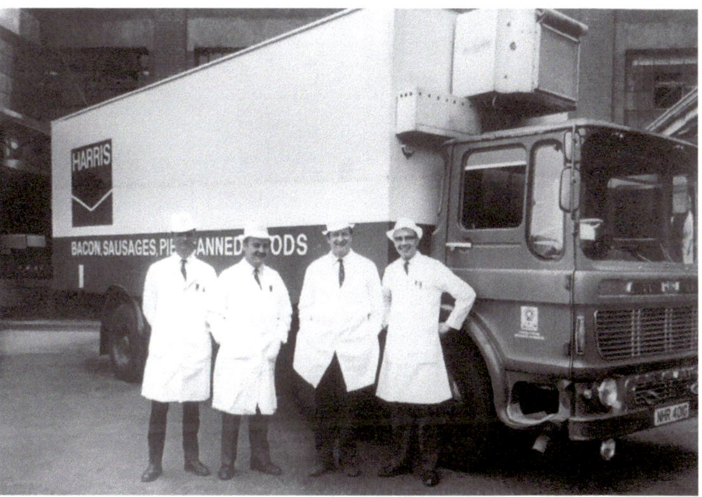

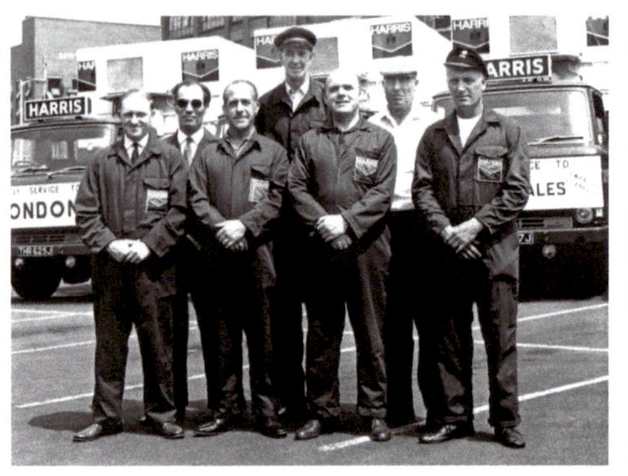 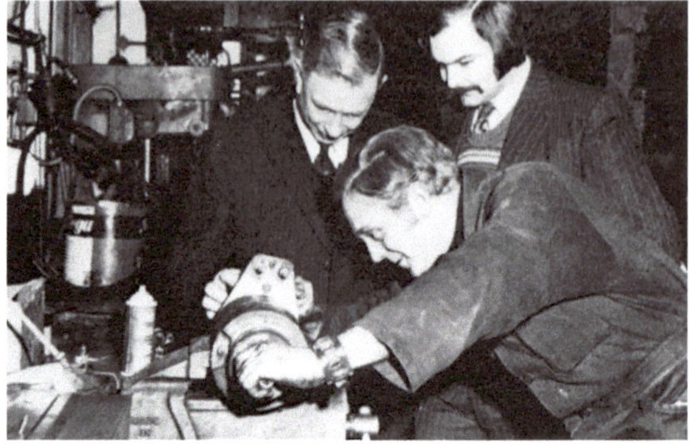

Above left: Harris drivers, left to right: Alan Townsend, Bill Ellis, Les Bullock, George Broome, 'Binky' Smith, Charlie Reeves and Wally Axford. The trucks appear to be Ford D Series, and the 'J' registration indicates 1970 /71.

Above right: Audley Coombs, fitter (front), Walter Hyde, chief engineer (left), and Mike Reynolds, transport engineer, working on a starting motor, Blue Rosette (Transport), Calne. *FMC News*, 1974.

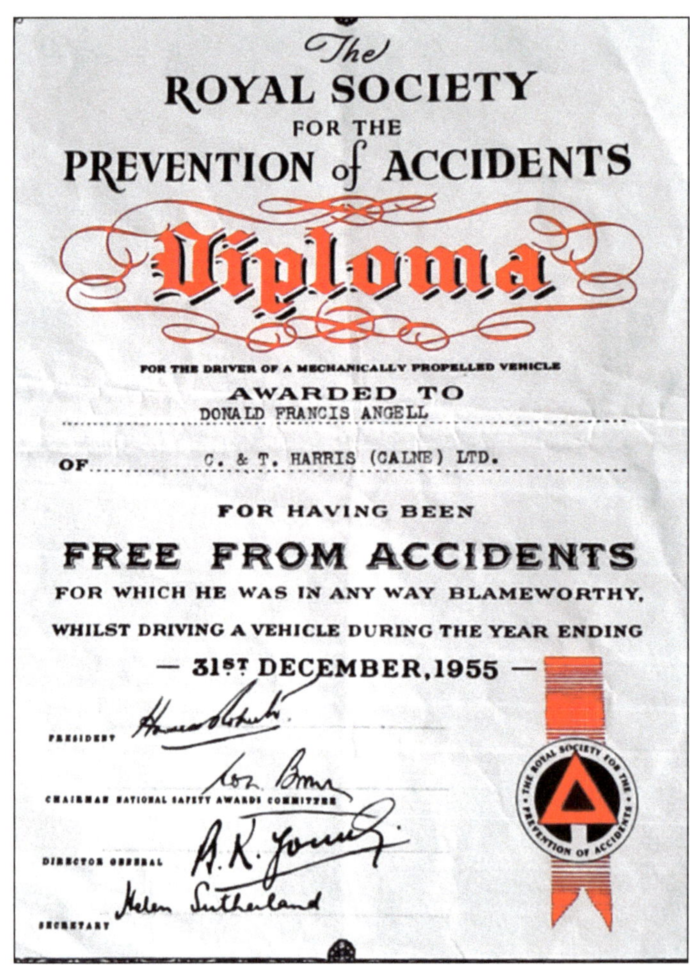

The Royal Society for the Prevention of Accidents Diploma – Free From Accidents for a Year, was awarded to Harris driver Donald Angell, 31 December 1955. (Mary-Ann Angell)

5

Early Working Life

'Many of the workmen, engaged in the industry wear long blue smocks and clogs;
consequently, at certain times of the day, the streets assume quite a blue tint, and the
pavements echo with the clang of the wooden shoon.'

A. E. W. Marsh, *A History of the Borough and Town of Calne*, 1903

Thanks to John Bodinnar, who established the monthly *Harris Magazine* (1927–40), we
learn a good deal about life at C. & T. Harris and its branches. Henry (Harry) Carpenter
(1849–1940), who worked at Harris for seventy years, was interviewed in 1930:

I started work for the late Mr Thomas Harris when I was ten years old and was paid
five shillings a week. There were fifteen men and two boys. At that time 100 pigs
were considered a heavy week in killing. The other branch of the firm employed more
hands but we worked quite independently.

I was a donkey boy for two years, taking meat round the villages, the joints packed
into panniers, thrown across the donkey's back on either side. I didn't ride the donkey.
I walked and came home pretty well tired out. On Saturday night I had to serve in the
shop which was always closed properly at 11 o'clock, after which I received my wages
and trudged home to Quemerford.

I was transferred to the Lard Room where I worked my way up from junior to
second hand and later Foreman. My wages increased by increment to *6d* a time to
15*s* 6*d* a week.

Hours weren't counted in them days. We kept at it till the work was done. The
longest day I ever worked was 20 hours from three in the morning till eleven at night.

I nearly got the sack once. I and my boy had to move a quantity of bladdered lard
stored on the floor above the old ICE house. It was a sitting down job and we both
fell asleep. Mr Harris and Foreman John Haddrell came up to see how work was
progressing. I was awakened by the master stirring me with his foot.

'Come, come, I pay you to work not to sleep. Sleep at home, not here.'

The time we had at home was hardly sufficient for a full night's rest and indeed
that was the simple truth. Every morning the 'caller' came around, tapping with his
stick on the old iron pipe on the side of my house and telling me it was half past
three. Time to get up.

Work from four in the morning and out at eight at night six days a week.

We had two days holiday – Christmas Day and trip day. For Christmas every
man was given a meat ticket to spend in the shop, the value according to the family
responsibilities of the recipient. Changes have been gradual but always for the better.

I well remember when the first steam engine was installed for pumping water and grinding fat, how we welcomed the lightening of the manual labour.

In the early days, the pigs were burnt with straw and then carried into the slaughterhouse on the men's backs. We were paid extra – 1½ *d* for every two pigs. Strict accounts were kept and the extra payment came as a sort of bonus, say for carrying 30 pigs – was 1*s* 10*d*.

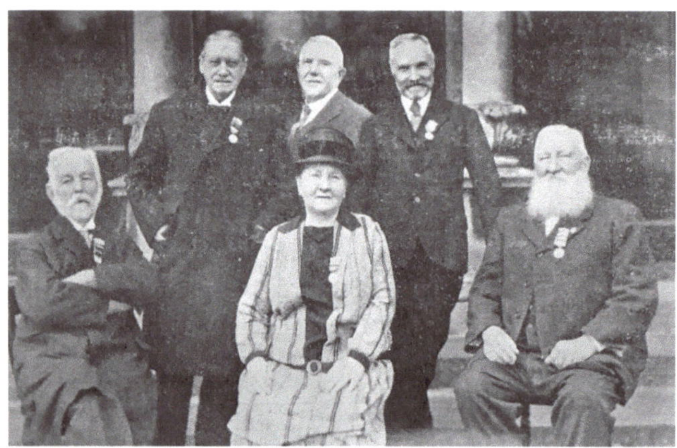

Celebrating long service, 1930. Left to right, standing: E. H. Weston (senior clerk) sixty-two years; J. Holley (Bacon Department) fifty-seven years; and J. Carpenter (senior clerk) fifty-seven years. Seated: W. Frayling (cashier) sixty-five years; Mrs Emma Carter (Bacon Department) fifty; and Henry Carpenter (lard maker) seventy years.

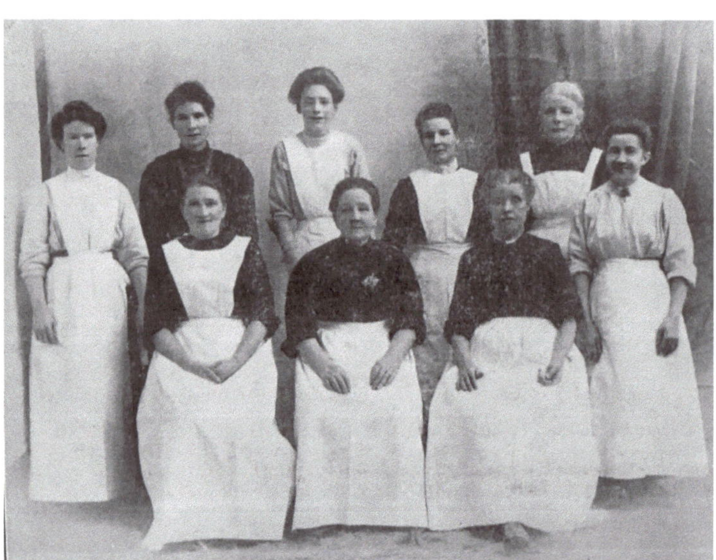

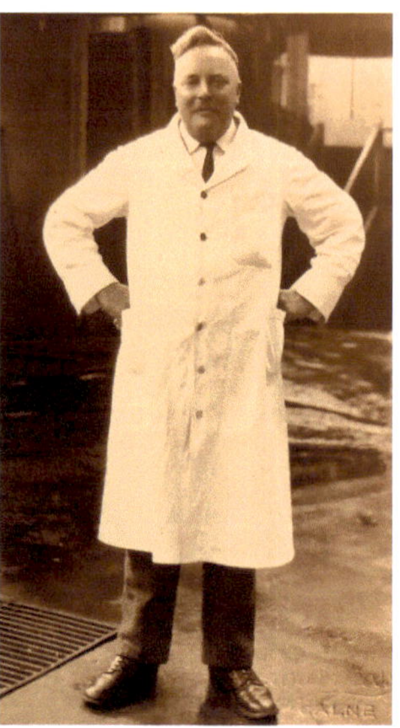

Above left: Women of the Boning Department, 1912. Back row, left to right: Mrs Bezant, Mrs Batchelor, Miss Bennett, Mrs Bowman, Mrs Smart, Mrs J. Smart. Front row: Mrs Watkins, Mrs Emma Carter and Mrs Parfitt.

Above right: Jack Clark (1879–1928), No. 2 Factory Manager. A former pig farmer, he supplied pigs to Harris before joining the company. After his death, John Bodinnar asked his widow Edith if she would hold the funeral at the weekend because so many employees wanted to attend. (Chris Hughes)

Another person of note was Mrs Emma Carter (née Clack), who was 'one of the first wave of feminine invaders of the bacon curing industry'. She had a long career at Harris starting work in 1881, with William Brewer, foreman, along with three other women: Mrs Smart, Mrs Wharton and Mrs Duck. A century later, women were the majority of the workforce at Harris.

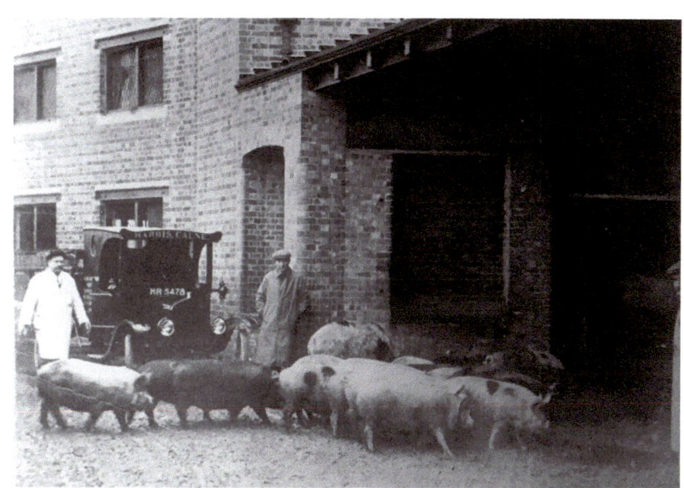

Right: Pigs arriving at the new slaughterhouse, 1920s.

Below: 'Guide when Ordering Bacon' illustration from *The Historic House of Harris* (1930s and 1940s) cookery pamphlet. Sides of bacon were branded with the Harris name with cast-iron brands heated in gas ovens.

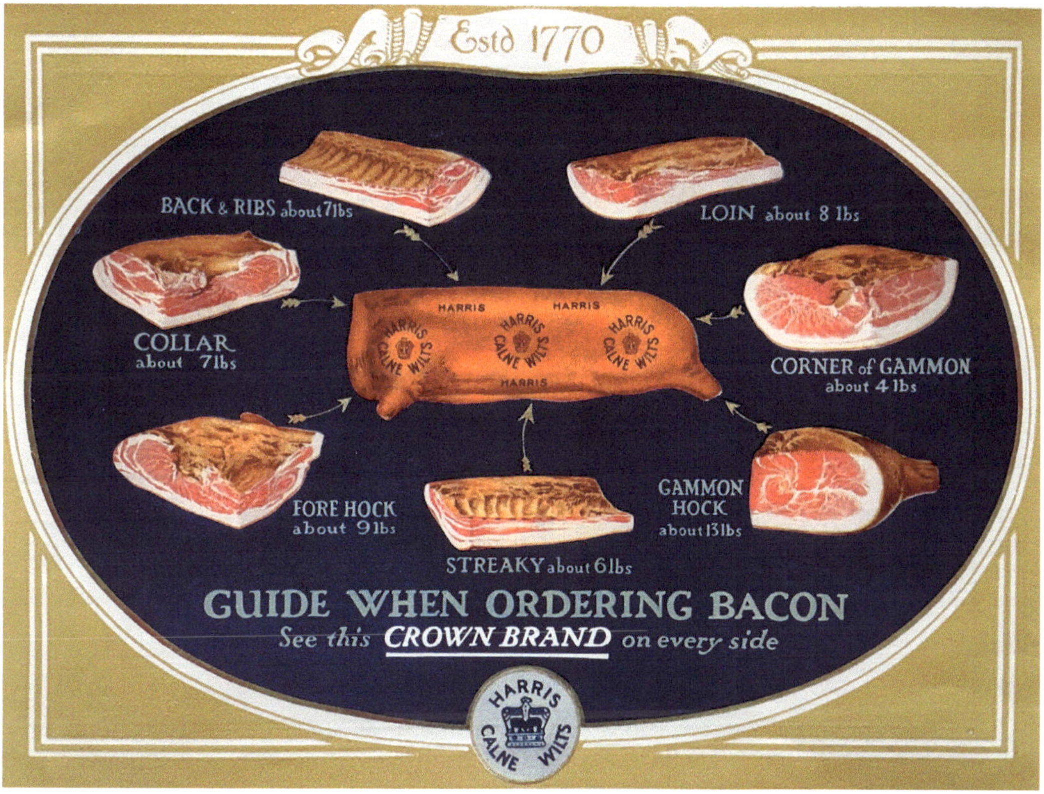

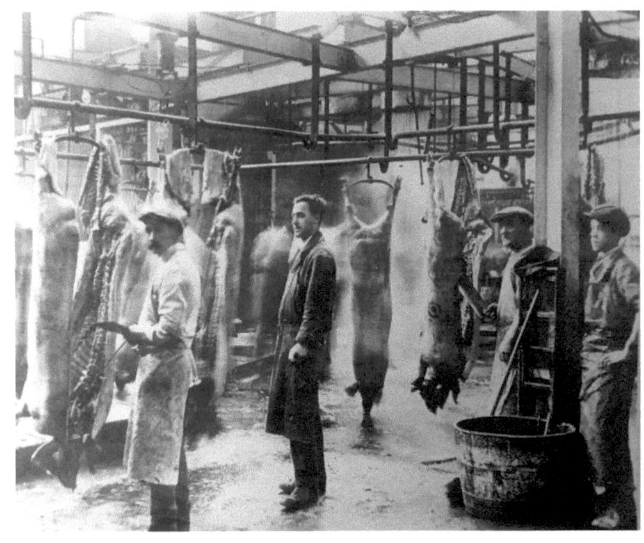

Butchery Department, splitting carcases, *c.* 1910.

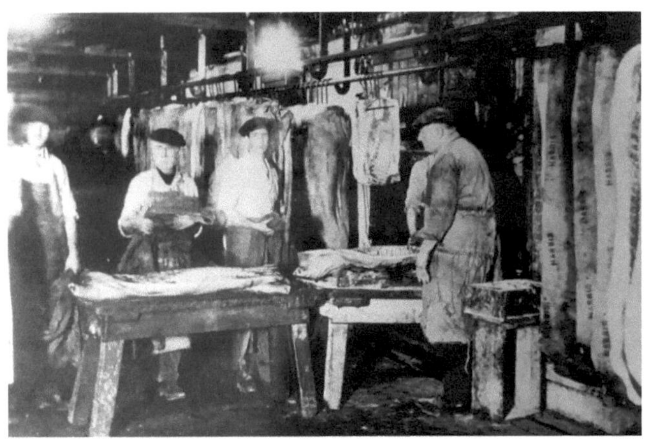

Preparing sides of bacon for smoking, rubbing in salt, *c.* 1910.

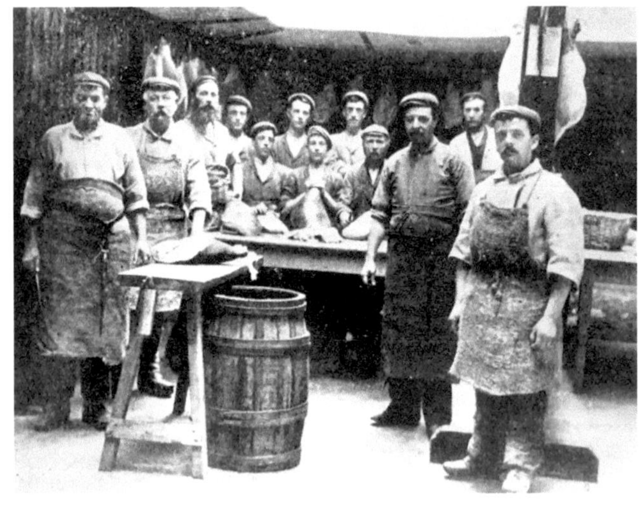

Ham Curing and Finishing Department, 1904. Left to right: R. Biffin, T. Hillier, J. Cleverly, H. Blackford, H. Boase, C. Knight, A. H. Haines, W. Garraway, W. Newth , W. R. Weston, F. Mitchell and J. Smart.

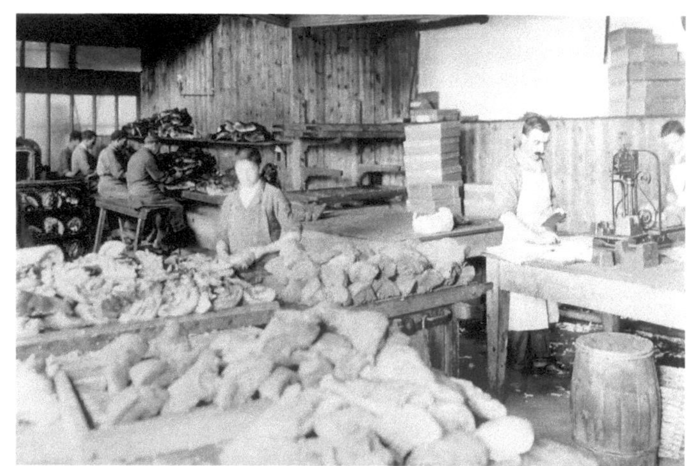

Salting and weighing joints, *c.* 1910.

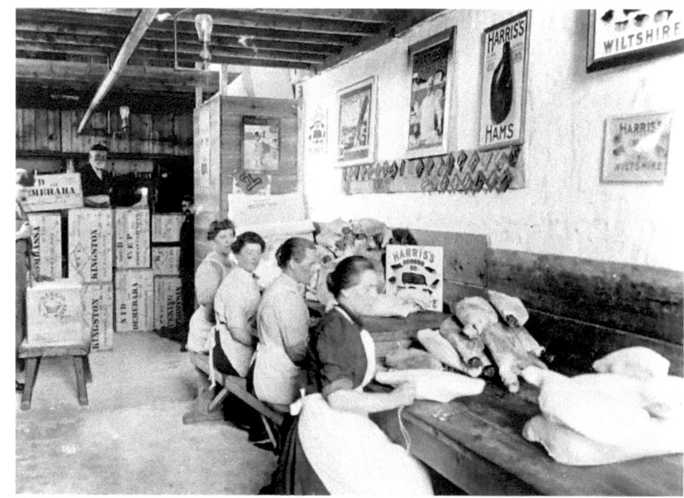

Women workers netting hams in hessian and stitching with string. The packing cases going overseas are labelled Kingston, Peking, Mombasa, Demerara, Port Swettenham (Port Klang), *c.* 1900.

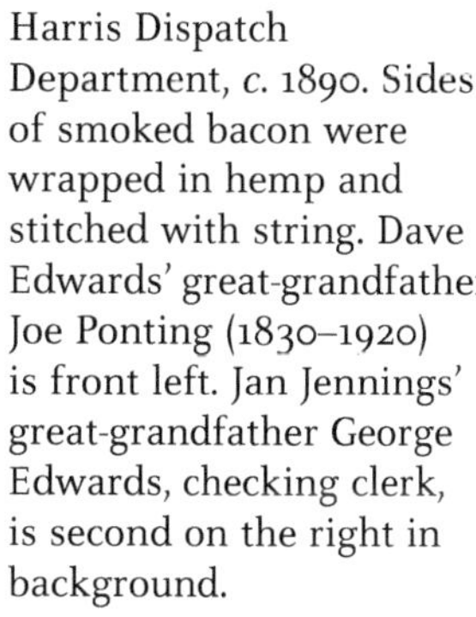

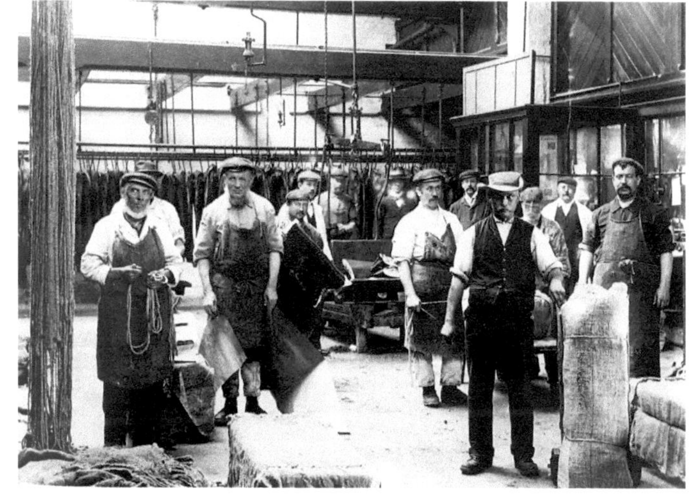

Harris Dispatch Department, *c.* 1890. Sides of smoked bacon were wrapped in hemp and stitched with string. Dave Edwards' great-grandfather Joe Ponting (1830–1920) is front left. Jan Jennings' great-grandfather George Edwards, checking clerk, is second on the right in background.

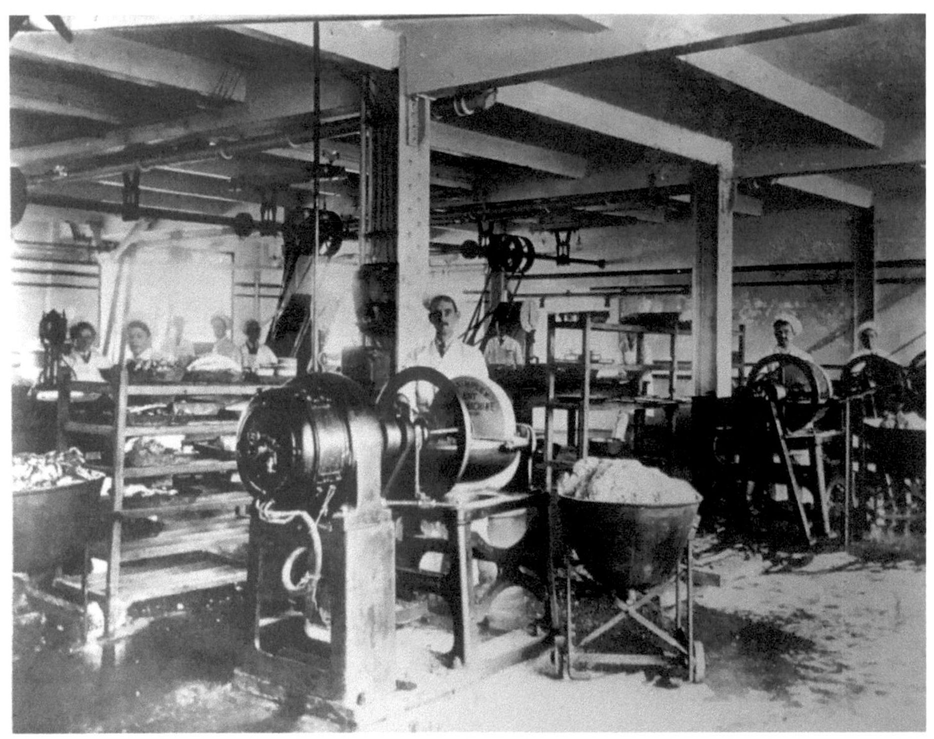

Mincing meat for sausages, *c.* 1910.

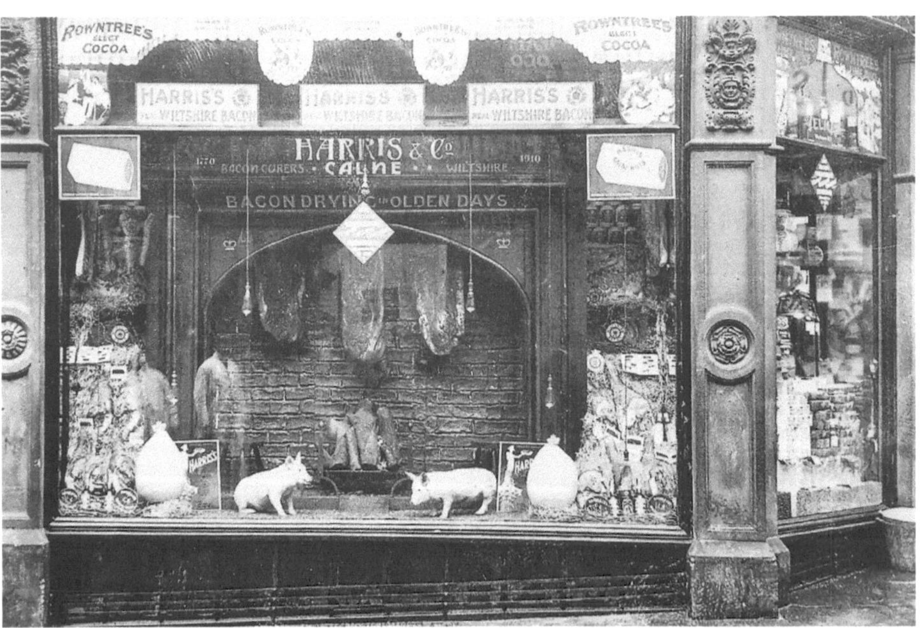

Harris retail shop, Church Street, 1910.

6

A Factory Tour, 1963, and By-products

From Pig to Pie

In order to get a flavour of a day in the life of the factory, a century on from Harry Carpenter, let's join a group of visitors at an open day in March 1963. Let's see what goes on behind the scenes.

No. 2 Factory Tour (Killing, Curing, Cutting, etc.)

Lairage

Pigs arrive any time during the day and night and are received at the lairage – holding pens here in The Pippin, so that there will be a steady flow of livestock to keep the slaughter line going. We can accommodate 1,500 pigs at a time, with extra facilities nearby. The buildings are well ventilated and large fans help to circulate the air and the facilities, where feeding and watering are available to the waiting pigs who need to rest for twenty-four hours before killing.

Gas Chamber

Carbon dioxide is used and the pigs are rendered unconscious after passing through the chamber on a moving belt. The whole process is automatic and the pigs emerge completely relaxed and ready for slaughter.

Slaughterhouse

We are not able to visit this part, owing to the nature of the work and for safety reasons because of machinery and conveyors. This is what happens to the pigs:

- Stunning by an electrical current (early methods were a blow to the head or the use of a bolt pistol).
- Hoisting up on gambrels – a frame shaped like a horse's hind leg, used by butchers for hanging carcases.
- Sticking – throat slitting by severing the jugular vein. The animal is left to bleed. The knife is sterilized as only used once.
- Blood is collected. Hygiene is important so that blood is not contaminated.
- Scraping, which is when skin is scalded and hair removed.

Dressing Bar

We are not able to access this enclosure where the carcases are held. Within this department scolding, de-hairing, singeing, scraping, marking down, which is when coloured labels are attached, splitting and de-gutting are carried out. The heads are also checked for TB, and other veterinary examinations are made.

Weighing and Grading

This is carried out by the Ministry of Food officials with Harris's own check weighers and recorders present. The scale is checked after every 100 pigs, each one certified with the producer's payment certificate. Our Harris employee measures the fat in three places along the back. Later, a probe is introduced in order to go deeper onto the carcase. The inspectors are looking for a nice lean pig as that receives higher subsidies from the government. Lean meat is more valuable than fatty ones. The best pigs are a cross between Swedish Landrace and English Large White (aka Yorkshire).

Veterinary Department

It is here that checks are made on the condition of both live and dead pigs to see that no diseased or contaminated meat shall be exposed for sale. Diseased and ailing live pigs are isolated and slaughtered when there is no risk of transferring infection to clean carcases or to equipment. We have had our own qualified veterinary surgeon and assistant since 1924.

We use a system of coloured labels on the carcases being dressed to indicate that special inspection is required. All diseased innards, pluck (heart, liver, windpipe, and lungs), etc., are then linked to the carcase from which they are taken.

The final examination decides the suitability of the whole or part of the carcase for human consumption.

Cutting Room

Here, the side is finally trimmed before going down into the tanks of brine below.

Dry Curing

In this section, specially selected sides are dry cured for the famous Harris Crown Brand Bacon. This is done through the injection of common salt and saltpetre, then copiously sprinkled and stacked. This process takes approximately twenty-one days.

Tank Cure or Mild Cured

The majority of bacon nowadays is cured by this method, which takes only twelve to fourteen days.

Brine is pumped into the side under pressure, great care being taken to see that each side receives just the required amount. The sides are then immersed in tanks of brine for five days and later stored to mature and drain for approximately seven to nine days.

Pork Cutting

Carcases are broken down into cuts for the fresh pork trade. This is where our dissection unit works when dealing with carcases, which are the subject of a research programme.

Demonstration of the Intrascope

Here you can meet Harris's own geneticist, Mr J. L. Jollans, appointed last year. He is currently working with the intrascope, a new probe used to measure the back fat and rind thickness. This helps us to identify the ratio of muscle (pork meat) to fat.

Bacon Smoking and Packing

We can see where the green sides are hung in the smoke chambers for the smoking process, which takes approximately eight to ten hours. One smoke-producing unit serves several chambers and smoke can be controlled to exact requirements. Bacon packing also takes place here and the conveyers take the packed side to the loading point.

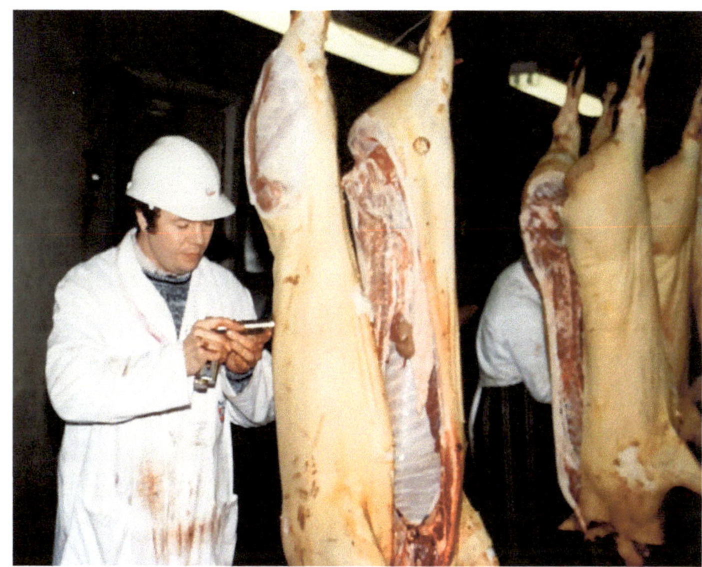

Harris Chippenham, Wiltshire Bacon Co., 1987. Using the intrascope, a probe to measure the back fat and rind thickness. (Ewart Taylor)

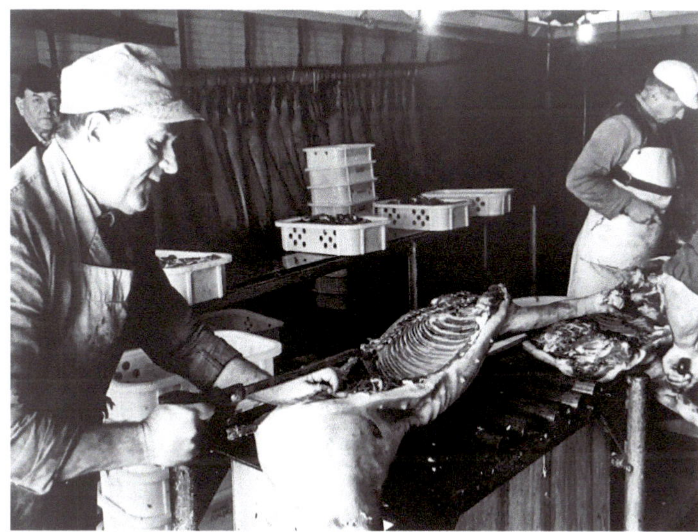

Butchery, 1968. John Meadows cutting a side of pork watched by Tony Livesey (corner left).

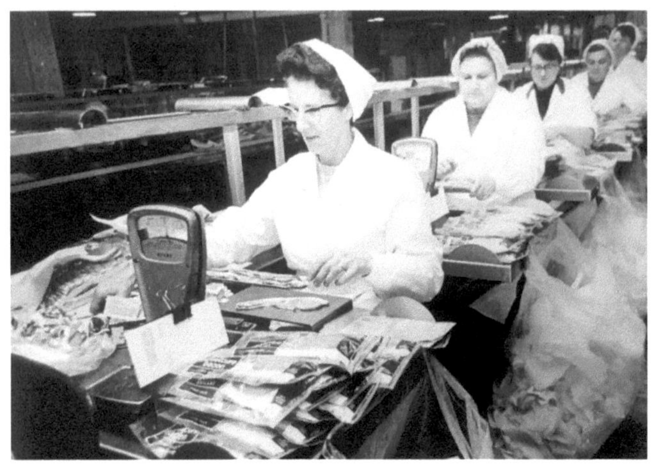

Weighing rashers of bacon before wrapping, 1968.

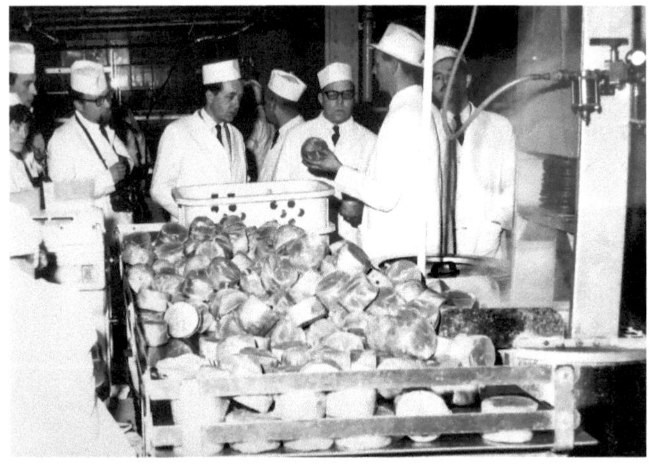

Dick Baggs, No. 1 Factory Manager, showing ham joints to visitors, 1952.

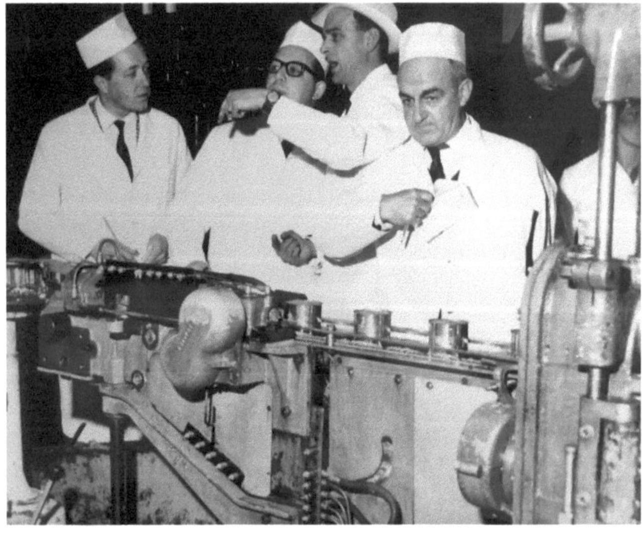

Dick Baggs, No. 1 Factory Manager, showing visitors a canning conveyor belt, 1950. Harris started canning during the First World War as a convenient way to store surplus meat. Cans were originally made by hand by tinsmiths employed locally.

No. 1 Factory (St Dunstan) Tour (Small Goods Production)

We start at the main gates, where you will see our uniformed commissionaire who oversees the yard. Proceed to the elevator.

Top floor – Kitchen

This is mainly devoted to the cooking and processing of a wide variety of Harris cooked meat products such as cooked ham, cooked shoulders, roast leg of pork, luncheon sausage, brawn, Bath Chaps, black puddings, etc. Also in this department meats are prepared and processed for canning.

Third floor – Canning

The equipment here is the most up-to-date high-speed canning machinery, capable of handling many hundreds of tins an hour. After filling and seaming, the cans are processed in retorts (sterilising vessels), then passed on to the packing lines where they are filled into cartons for disptach. Lines such as savoury mince, steak and kidney pudding, hamburgers, baconburgers, luncheon meat and chopped cured pork are produced here.

Third floor – Laboratory

This is our new Chemical and Bacteriological Laboratory. Raw materials used in the various manufacturing processes are examined here together with our finished products including sausages, pies, bacon, cooked meats and canned goods. The tests are made to confirm that raw materials and finished products comply with the requirements of the Food and Drugs Act and also that the high standards set for our goods are maintained.

Constant checks in the Bacteriological Laboratory ensure that our products leave the factory absolutely fresh and in acceptable condition. A full-time hygiene officer works alongside laboratory staff to ensure that a close watch is kept on hygiene standards throughout the factory.

Second floor – Boning Department

All the various types of meat are prepared here for the manufacturing departments. You can see meat for canning sausages and making pies being carefully boned, sinewed, trimmed, and cut up to the precise specification for each product. Also, bacon is boned and prepared for our Pre-pack Bacon Factory.

Second floor – Sausage Department

This department is engaged full time in the production of pork and beef sausages of various sizes both for home and export markets. All sausages are manufactured to a special formula, which is rigidly adhered to in order that Harris sausages are always of high quality and consistent in texture and flavour.

First floor – Printing Department

Here you can see the printing machines, which produce price lists, invoices, letter headings, printed office stationery, cardboard boxes, etc.

First floor – Lard Department
This is where surplus fats are rendered into Harris Lard, which is filled into half-pound packets, bladders and 28-lb-bulk packs.

15A & 15B Ground floor – Pie Department
A wide range of Harris pies of different sizes and varieties are produced here. In the pastry room, flour and fat are carefully kneaded and the dough passed into the Pie Room to be formed into meat pies. One of the main features here is the continuous travelling oven, capable of baking 3,500 small pies per hour. After baking, pies are cooled and jelly is injected into the air holes. The pies are cooled again, packed and dispatched.

Ground floor – Warehouse
Harris products are assembled in accordance with orders, for dispatch to our customers and van salesmen throughout the country.

Ground floor – Dispatch
You can see Harris vehicles being loaded. A fleet of thirty-five lorries leaves the factory daily for destinations all over the country.

Basement – Small Goods Cellar
Various types of meat are cured in special brines to a high standard required for use in Harris products. In particular, for meats for brawn, pressed brisket of beef, ox tongues, Bath Chaps, hams, etc.

Our tour ends here.

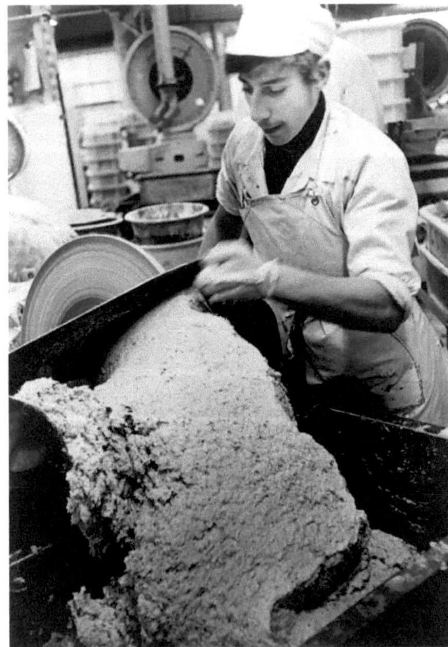

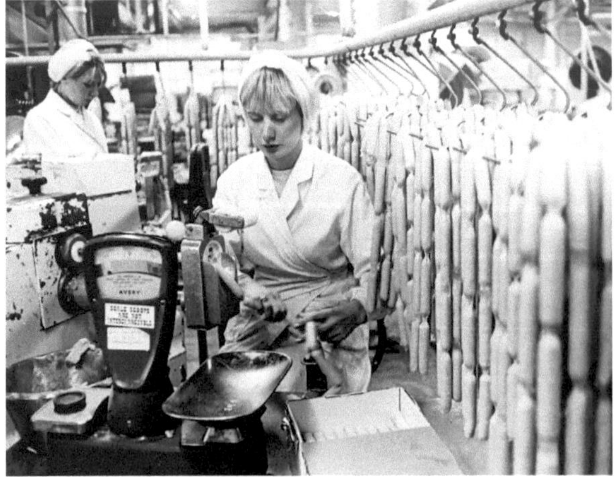

Left: Peter Cole handling a never-ending supply of sausage meat, 1968.

Below: Pat Marshall weighing batches of sausages before packing, 1968.

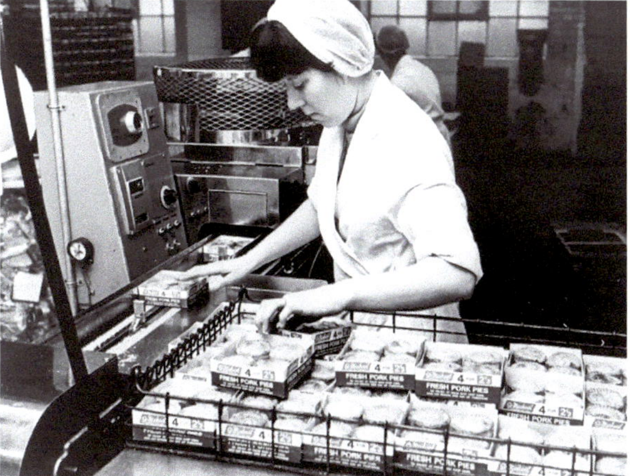

Above: Boxes of pork pies for Marks & Spencer (brand name St Michael) being wrapped in cellophane, 1968.

Right: Record of alteration to M&S recipe for puff pastry for sausage rolls, 1960.

ALTERATION IN RECIPE.

Pie Dept.

DATE 24 | 11 | 1960   N° 701

ARTICLE Marks & Spencer Duff Pastry for Sausage Rolls

Commence 25 | 11 | 1960

	Lbs.	Ozs.	Drms.
Heygates Flour	140		
Lard	17	8	
Salt		14	
Cream of Tartar	1	10	
Water	65		
Pastry Margarine	70		

METHOD: Mix Flour, Cof Tartar and Salt – Add Lard and Mix for 2 Minutes. Add cold water and Mix to Stiff Paste. Cut Dough into 16 lb pieces and Roll or Knead into 24" Squares. Fold Pastry over Margarine (5 lbs), which is placed on Top. Stand for 1 Hour.

REMARKS 3. Half Turns. Rest Overnight. Then 3 Half Turns, Then Roll For use. To Each Sausage Roll: 1 oz (App) Piece of Pastry measures 4" x 3½"

SIGNED ___________

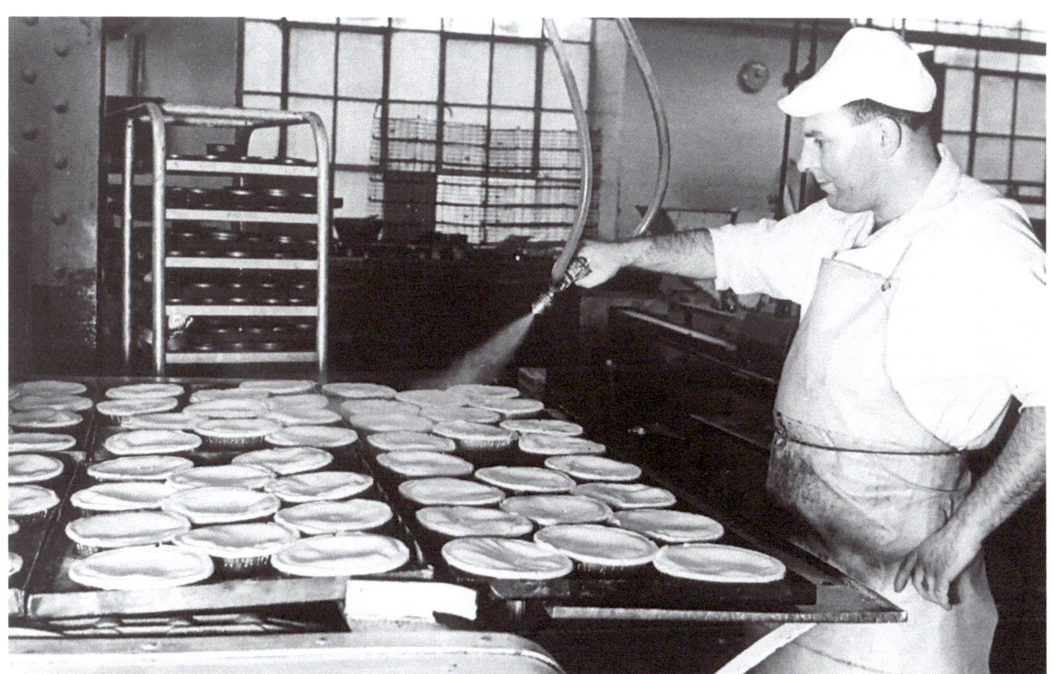

Pie Room, 1968. Oliver Burchill spraying water on steak and kidney pies before baking. He left school to work at Harris's, did two years National Service, which didn't break his service for the company, and was made redundant in 1981/82.

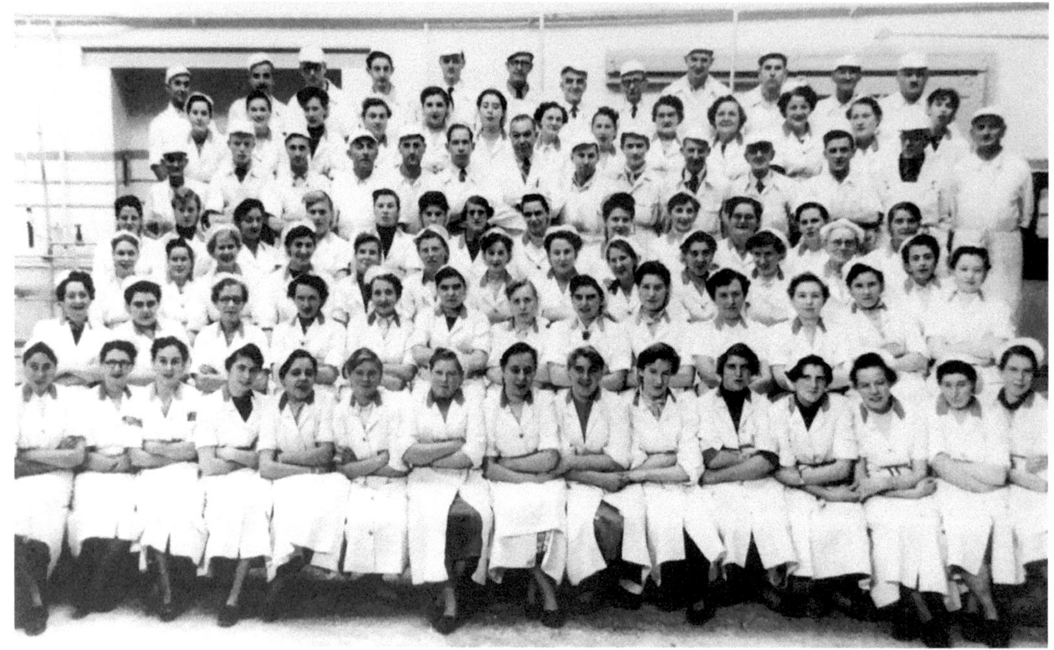

Harris Pie Department group photo, 1952/53.

What was not included in the Factory Tour was what happened to all the leftover bits, not fit for human consumption.

By-products

'By-products are known in the trade as "the fifth quarter".' FMC report, 1976.

Waste meat, bone and blood were valuable commodities. Every leftover part of the animal found a home in another product, from snout to tail – everything but the squeak. Sausage casing from guts, brushes from bristles, and glue from hooves and bones. Curled hair was used to stuff mattresses and car upholstery, dried blood for animal feed, bone meal for fertilisers, and fat turned into soap. Pharmaceutical manufacturers used by-products for medical purposes, such as insulin from the pancreas, and hormone treatments from pituitary glands.

'Originally,' John Bromham wrote, 'a mix of meat and bone was boiled in a steam-heated, vertical cylindrical vessel locally known as The Devil, on account of the offensive smells emanating therefrom.' From 1918 to 1930 the Bone and Tallow Department was situated at No 2. Factory adjacent to the river.

A separate by-products factory was built in 1930 at Wenhill, opposite the railway station; it had a boiler house and incinerator. In 1940, a fat refinery was built alongside, where crude fat was pumped over and processed into a completely sterile, odourless

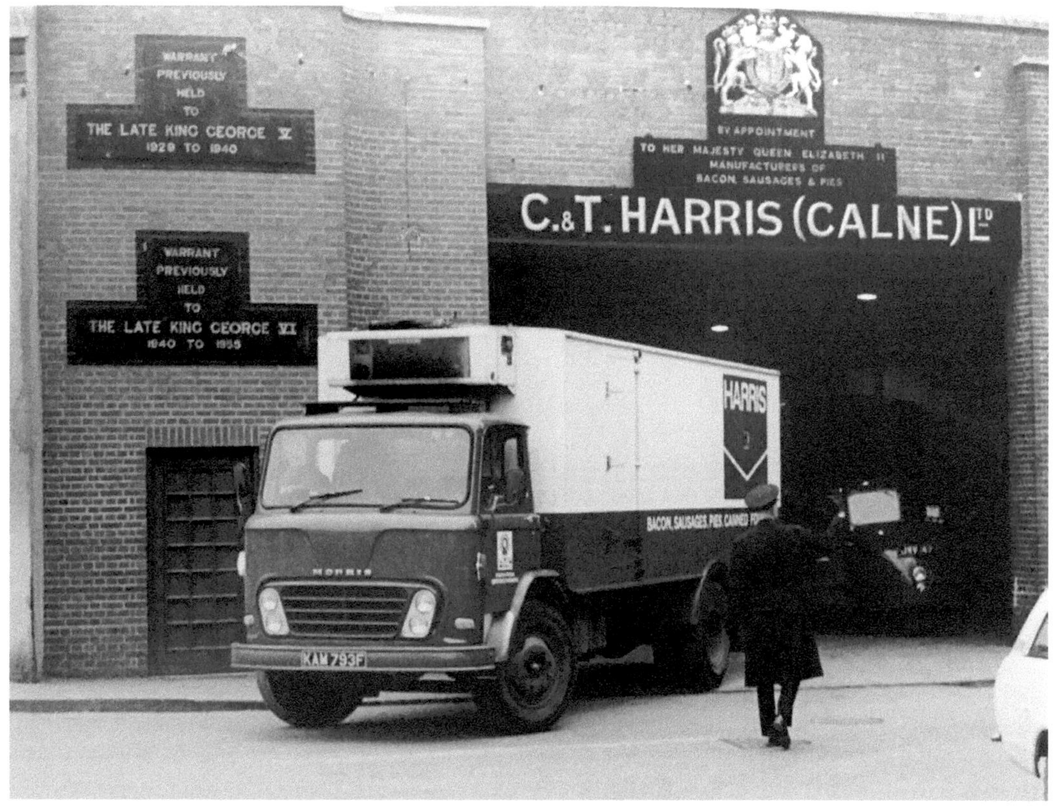

Harris refrigerated lorry leaving dispatch area, Church Street. Two royal warrants from George V and George VI, and Royal Arms by Appointment to HM Queen Elizabeth II, proudly displayed on the building, 1968.

and tasteless product. This 'grease' would be used by various industries, including cosmetics.

FMC, who took over in 1962, owned a number of subsidiaries specialising in hides and skins, for example, which were processed and sold to UK leather manufacturers. Most of the pelts, according to a 1976 report, were pickled, which meant that they could be sent overseas.

No one who lived or worked in Calne could forget the stench from by-products, especially in warm weather. The factory (run by Menzies) was forced to close in 1978 as a response to local pressure.

7

Advertising and Packaging

'So fresh, so tempting, so time-saving – prepared with all the traditional skills for which Harris foods are renowned.'

(1956 advert)

With their distinctive lettering, crown symbol and royal coat of arms, C. & T. Harris goods were instantly recognisable. They had been supplying royal households since Queen Victoria, the royal warrants passing down the line to George V, George VI and Elizabeth II. Harris enjoyed showing off the insignia and blowing its own trumpet about awards and prizes.

Everything, from sides of bacon to vehicles and franking marks on letters usually bore the company name and crown, followed by the ubiquitous slogan 'famous since 1770'. Even wagons of Harris products leaving Calne station, Graham Tanner records in *The Calne Branch*, had special yellow side plates, together with roof boards labelled in bold black letters 'Harris's Wiltshire Sausages'. Another way to keep the Harris brand in the public eye.

Storytelling and nostalgia for a golden age were two of Harris's key elements in advertisements. There were booklets such as *The Historic House of Harris* published in the 1920/30s, telling the Harris story, illustrated with pictures of workers in various departments and accompanied by striking colour illustrations of products.

Posters, show cards, labels and packaging were produced in the Printing Department. Van salesmen distributed price lists, information about new products and advertising material to retail outlets. Harris exhibited at shows and exhibitions across the country, displaying a huge array of produce, spreading the word and attracting new customers. Cookery demonstrations and tastings attracted the crowds; fry-ups were very popular.

Harris advertised regularly in national newspapers and women's magazines. For the last two decades the focus shifted to ready meals as well as the traditional favourites – bacon, sausages and pork pies. There were campaigns to attract families with novelty gifts: piggy banks, the 'Bangerang' launcher and special offers on watches.

Versions of the Harris history continued in the 1960s and 1970s with variations including 'Sweet cure of Wiltshire', 'How ice came from Norway before refrigeration was invented', and 'Harris Bring Back the Golden Age of English Food', which featured the pork pie:

Back in the 18th century, when men were trenchermen, pork pies were one of the glories of country cooking. Harris believe they still are. We make them as carefully now as we did in 1770. Crisp golden pastry, rich chopped pork, a hint of seasoning … that's a Harris pie for you. All ready to bite into.

The advertising campaign with the 'Deliciously old-fashioned' tagline, which ran from October 1971 to May 1972 , was presented to sales staff as 'a most unusual and memorable one and the most extensive advertising campaign we have undertaken.' It was bold in its approach, 'The message is right. The time is right. The sales will be right'.

In 1972/3, *FMC News* reported a national promotion for 'The Great British Breakfast' jointly with the Eggs Authority and Bacon Curers' Foundation. 'The TV commercials are supported by an intensive merchandising drive to identify stockists of British bacon and eggs and by a poster campaign in the Midlands.' Leaflets and recipes were distributed and special in-store promotions were organised, with the background smell of frying bacon.

Clive Van Hoek was appointed graphic designer from 1972 to 1980 by Bill Tullburg, marketing director. He worked on a number of projects including redesigning the Harris logo for a new generation, as well as changing the stationery. Clive remembers:

I often wondered why, when Sir John Stratton, his directors and advisors knew that the FMC group was failing, we spent a fortune on changing all the different companies' stationery, removing their logos and replacing them with the FMC blue rosette symbol. Many of the group members detested losing their individual company image, and let me know it!

1975 saw the 'Eat Meat' campaign followed by 'Love at first bite' and another packaging redesign in 1979. Sadly, no redesign, different slogan or new headed notepaper could save the company.

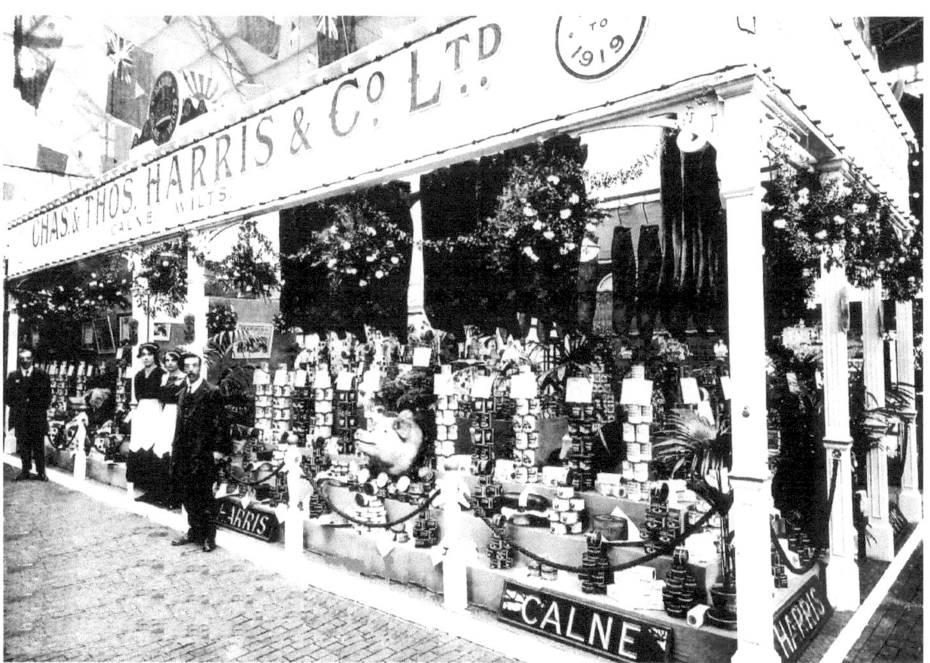

Harris display at a London show, possibly Smithfield, 1919. Jam-packed with goodies, including towers of tins, which may reflect their advances in canning at this time.

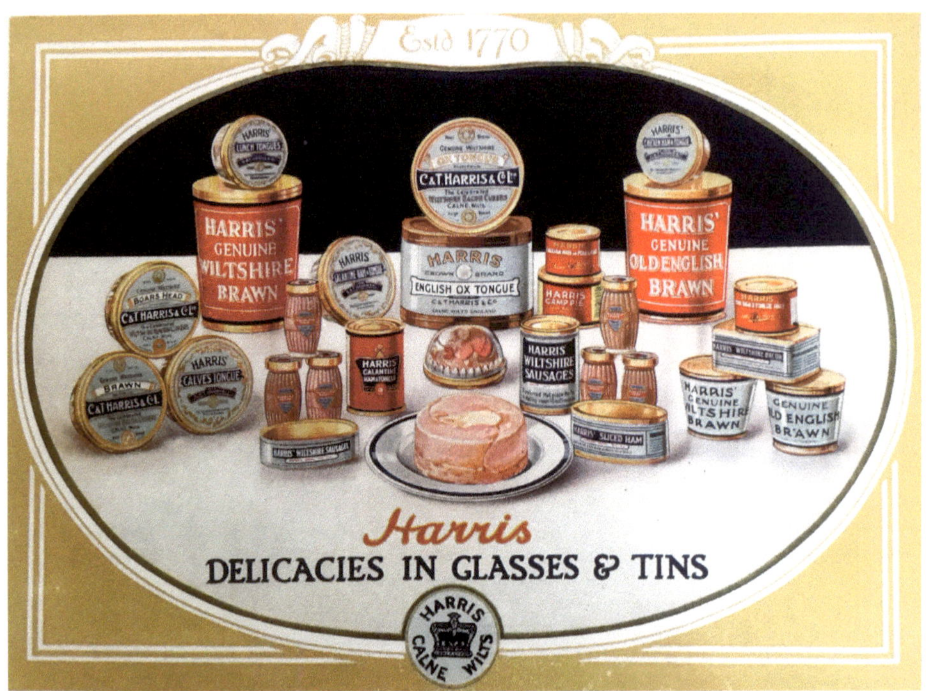

The range of Harris delicacies in glasses and tins from *The Historic House of Harris,* 1920s.

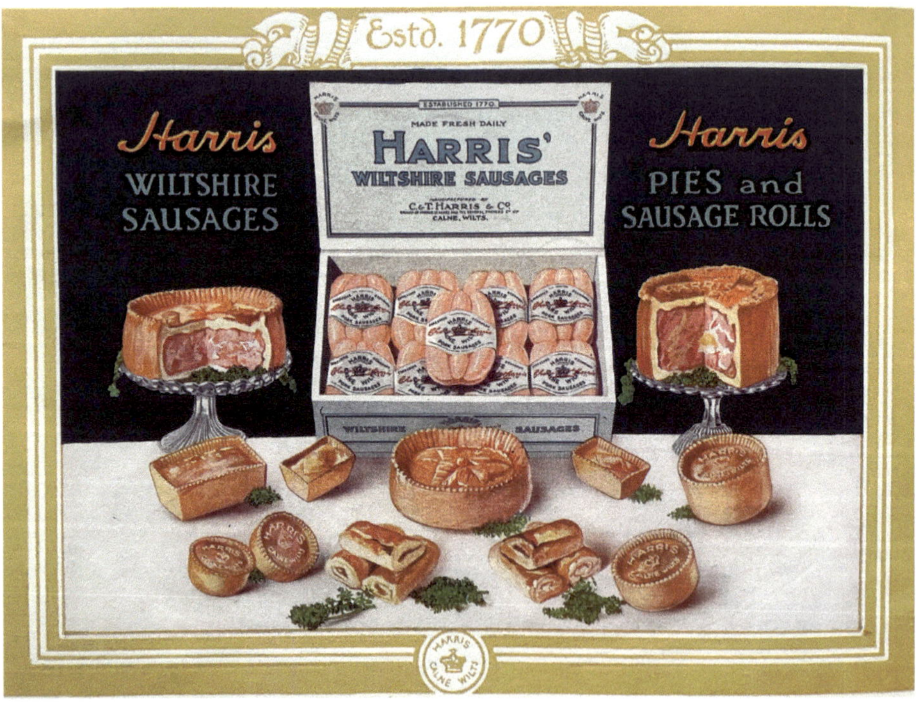

Harris sausages, pies and rolls advert, 1920s.

1930s labels. Pork cheese is another name for head cheese or brawn.

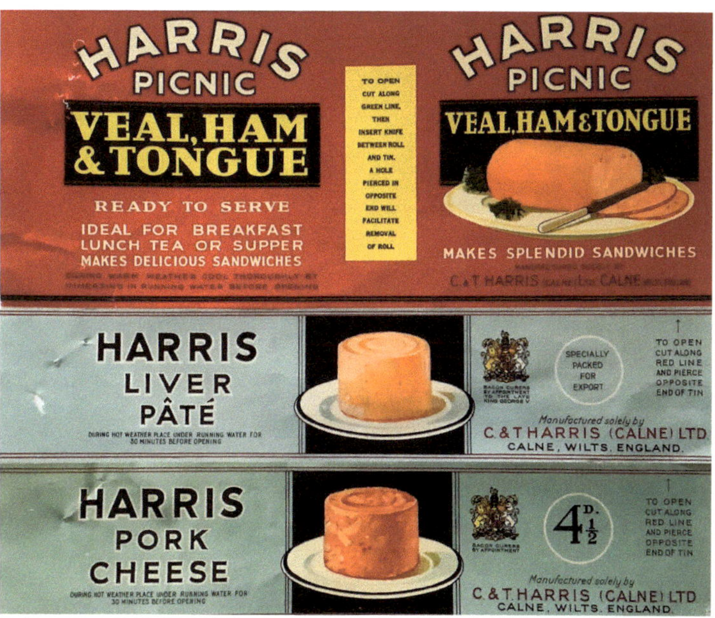

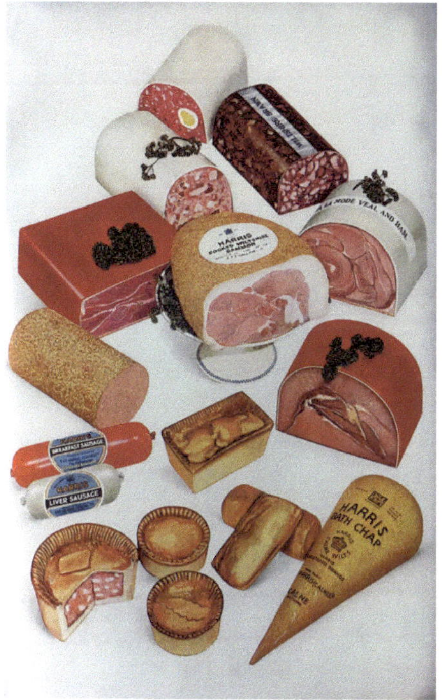

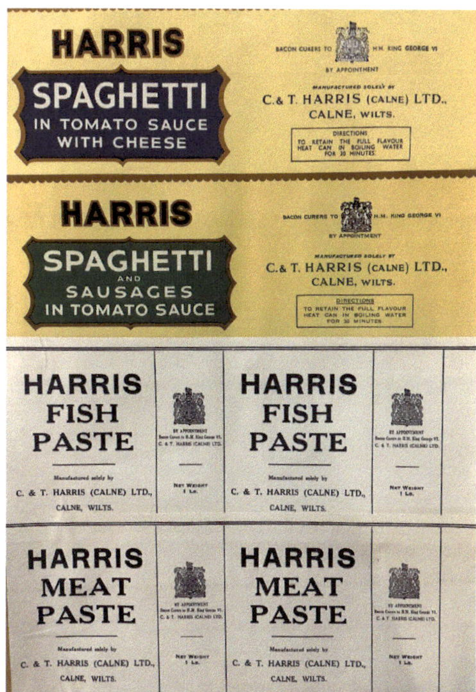

Above left: Illustration from *Keep House on Harris*, 1930/40s. Recipes include curried sausages, bacon kedgeree and jellied sausage mould. Bath Chaps (or cheeks) (bottom right) come from half the lower jaw of a pig's head, salt-cured like bacon and crumbed.

Above right: Labels for cans of spaghetti and jars of fish and meat paste, 1930/40s. (Wiltshire & Swindon History Centre, ref: 2140/116)

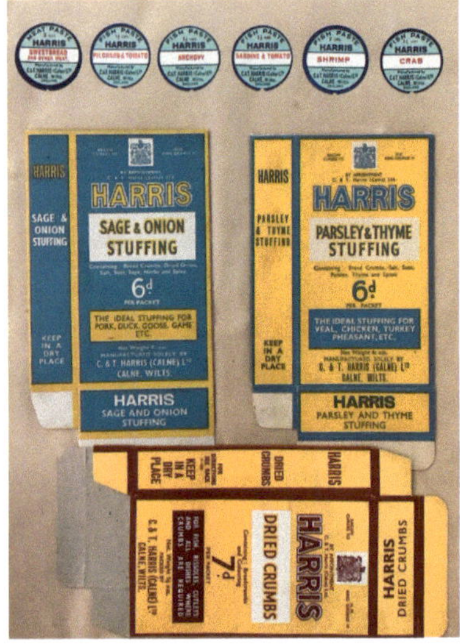

Left: Fish paste labels and stuffing packets, 1930/40s. (Wiltshire & Swindon History Centre, ref: 2140/116)

Below: C. & T. Harris at London Grocers' Exhibition, 1935.

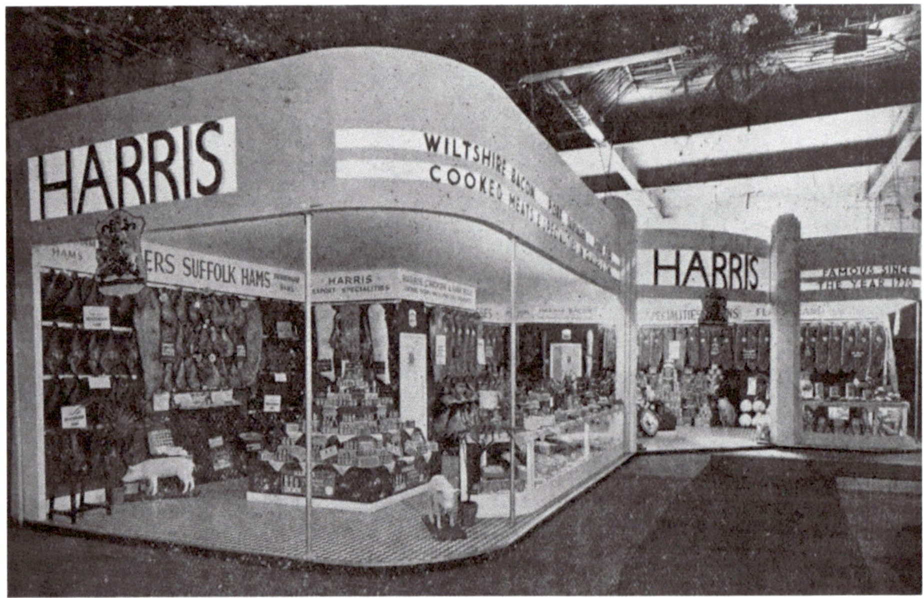

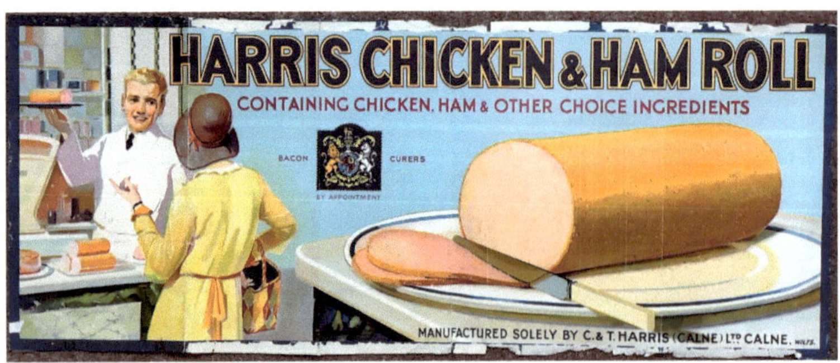

Shop banner/ window display for Harris Chicken & Ham Roll, 1937.

Right: Totnes Carnival Week, July 1938.
Harris's branch Bedford lorry decorated
for the Trade Section of the procession,
promoting 'John Bull's Breakfast'. For two
hours, a chef on top fried rashers of bacon
non-stop to feed their 'John Bull'.

Below: 'Get the Harris Habit' Christmas
promotion of Harris goods for retail shops,
c. 1960.

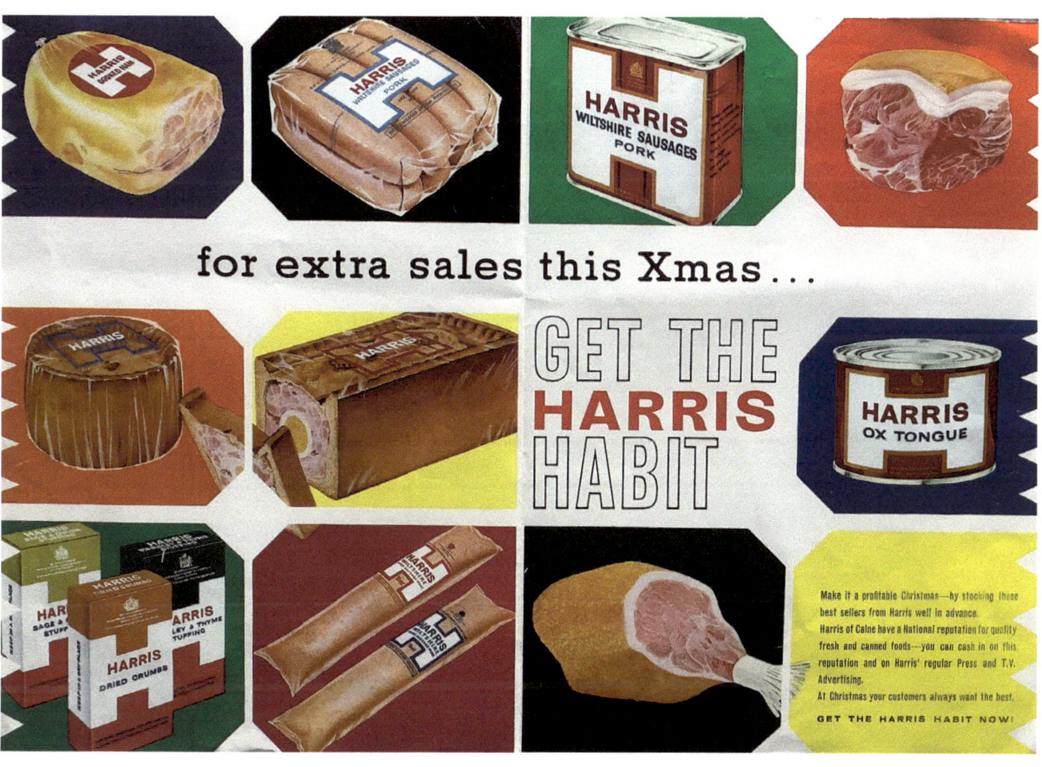

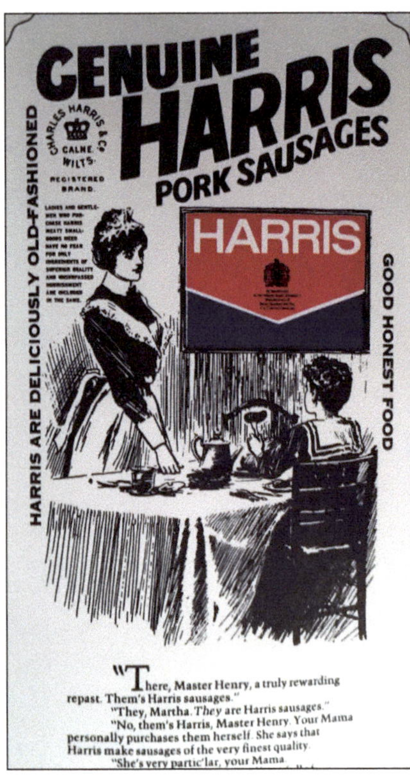

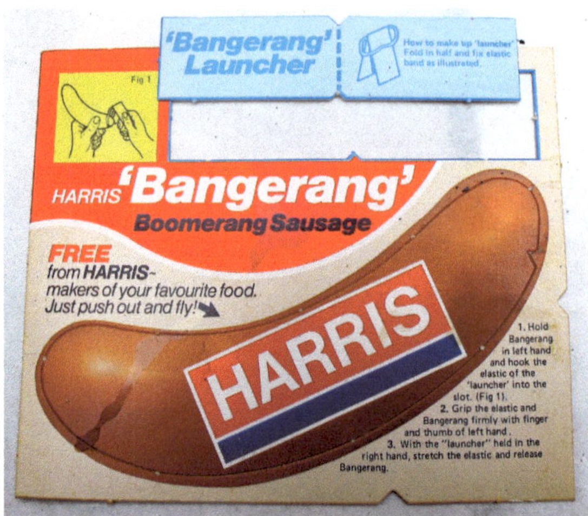

Above: Bangerang Launcher, promotional free gift for children, 1970s.

Left: From the 'Still deliciously old-fashioned' advertising campaign, October 1971–May 1972. 'There, Master Henry, a truly rewarding repast. Them's Harris sausages.' 'They, Martha. They are Harris sausages.' 'No, them's Harris, Master Henry. Your Mama personally purchases them herself.'

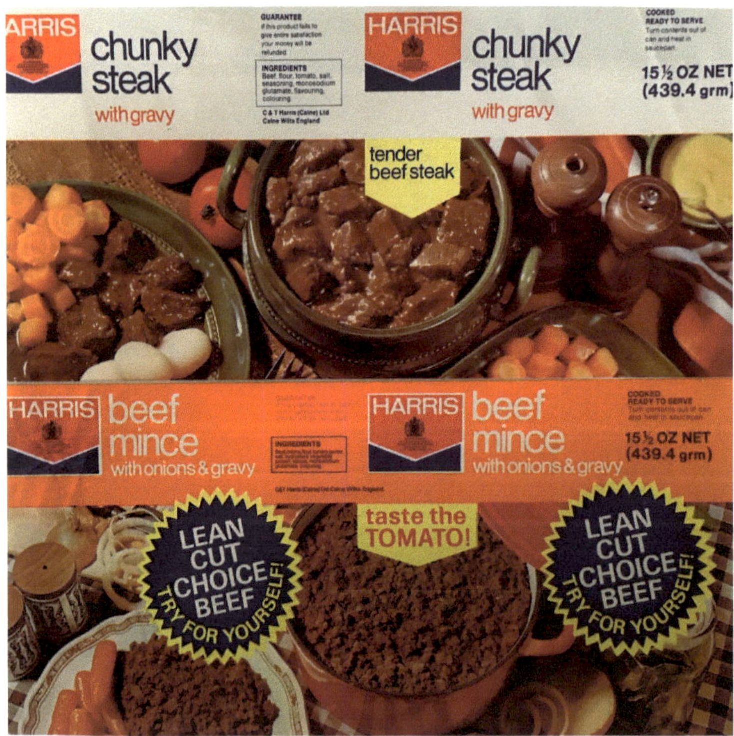

1970s labels from tins of chunky steak with gravy, and beef mince with onion gravy. Harris processed beef and chicken for a variety of ready meals.

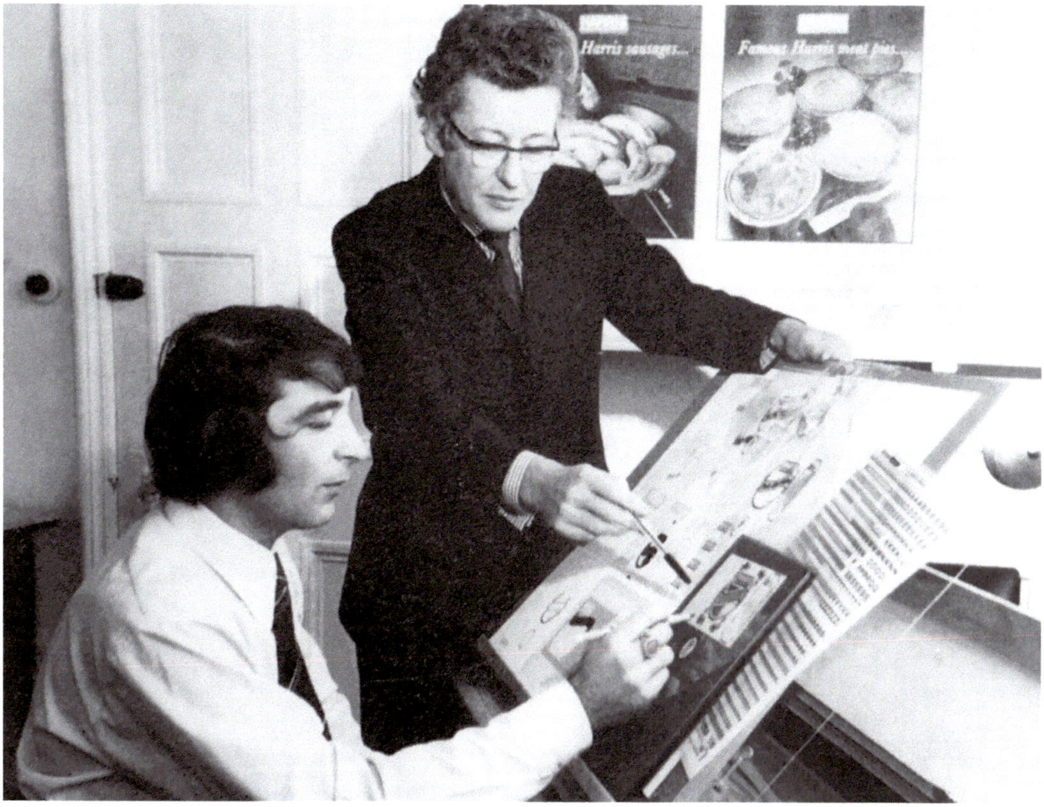

Above: Peter Heard, Purchasing Manager, with Clive Van Hoek, graphic designer (seated), 1974. Redesigning packaging, replacing the chevron logo with a narrower shape and rounded edges for a softer look. Clive is using Letraset, dry transfer sheets of typefaces.

Right: 'Harris Bring Back the Golden Age of English Food' advert, 1970s.

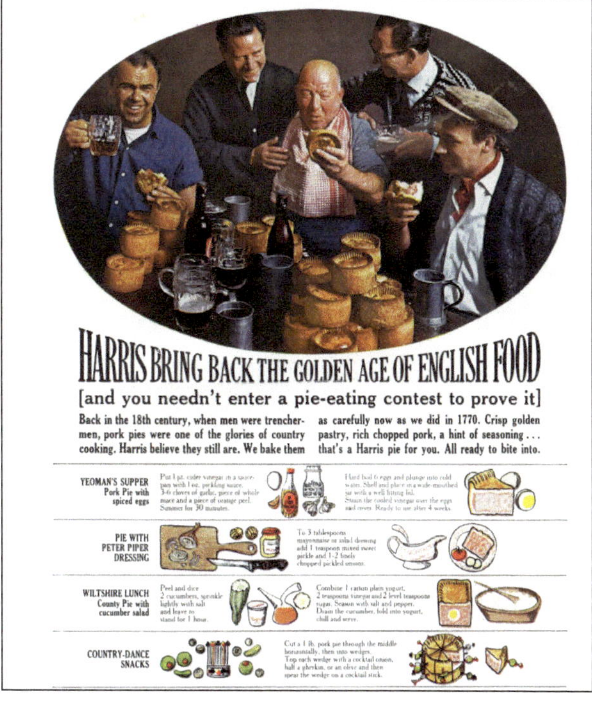

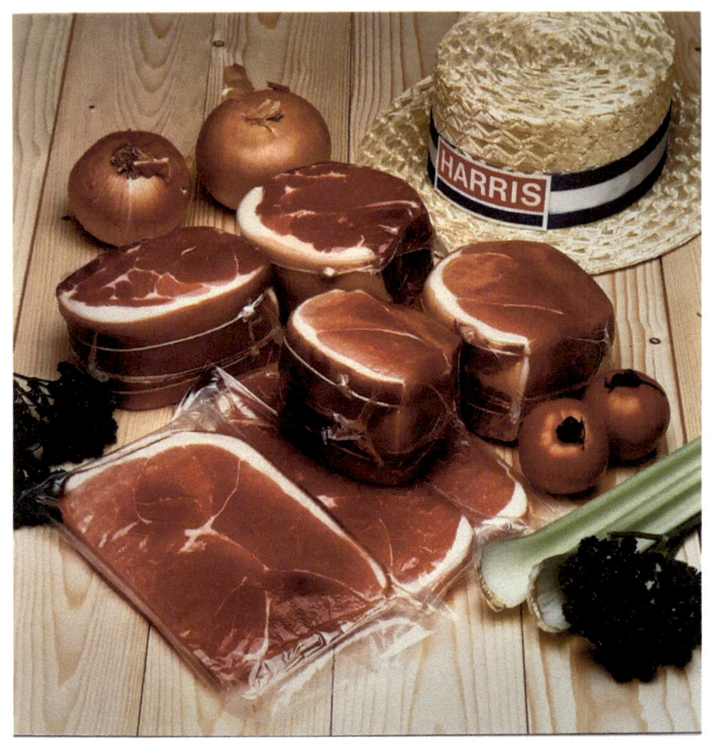

Left: A new style advert for cuts of bacon, late 1970s.

Below: A display of Harris Bacon at Harrods, 1979.

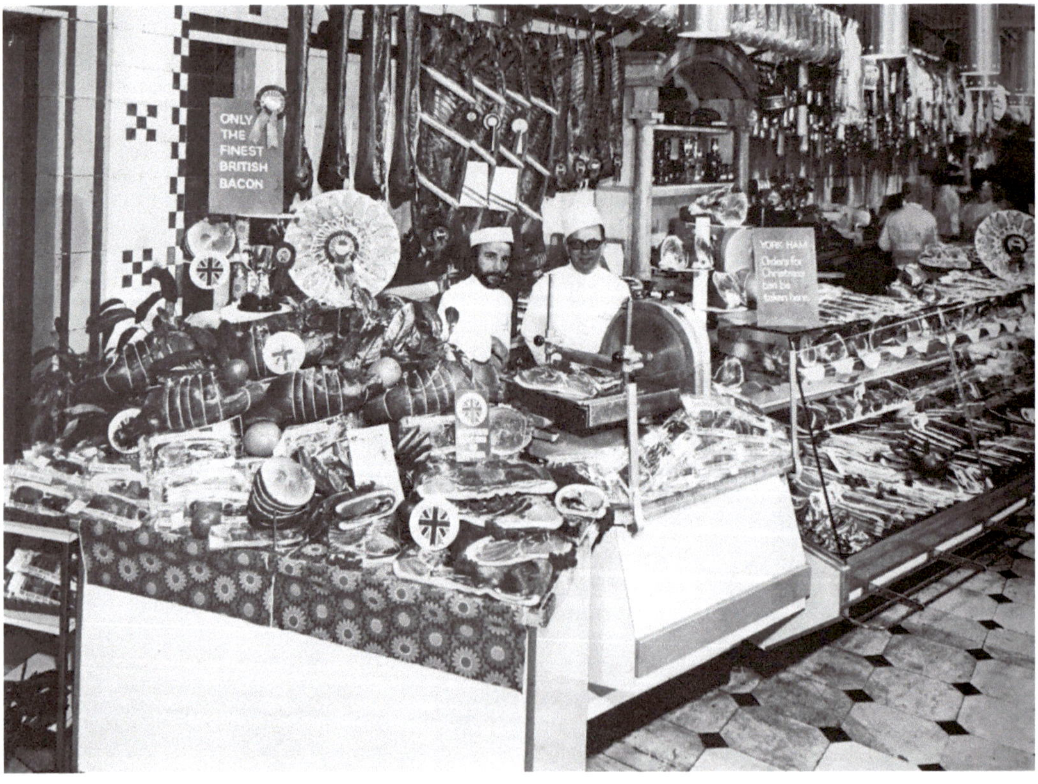

8

Down Memory Lane

Edward Spearey remembers his father Martin Spearey, Chief Engineer (1962–69):

Harris advertised for a new assistant to the Chief Engineer, which seemed like an ideal opportunity for my father. He had been working as a factory engineer at the Nestlé condensed milk factory in Chippenham, which was closing. Martin became the new assistant to Chief Engineer – John 'Jack' Bromham. Not long after he started, the day came when the new turbine had been run up to speed with the usual degree of discomfort on the way. Jack Bromham turned to Martin and said 'This is ridiculous – why don't you be the Chief Engineer and I will be your assistant' which is what happened. Martin had worked with steam turbines and power generating plant during his service in the Royal Navy between 1939 and 1953 so he was familiar with them.

One of the turbines had to be taken off load for a short time. This was usually done on Sunday mornings when the electrical load from the factory was at its lowest. The Howden engine would then be started up. One day father received a letter from the Rev Canon Douglas O'Hanlon, Vicar of St Mary's Church, asking if he could do something to stop the atrocious racket that seemed to break out in the factory just as he was starting his sermon at Matins. He requested him not to run the huge steam engine, which powered the Harris turbines, on a Sunday morning, as it rendered his sermon inaudible to the congregation.

Bob Bromham lived in Lickhill Road and remembers his daily walk to and from the Bentley Grammar School, passing where his father, Chief Engineer John Bromham, worked.

Like most children I went home for lunch and I passed along Church Street, and the entrance to the Harris boilers and power station – four times a day for eleven years. The sweating stokers shovelled coal into the fireboxes from the piles deposited by the trucks that brought it from the intermediate storage at the station. With the fire doors open, the raging furnace inside dominated the surroundings. Few shopping streets would have had this alien sight within their locale. This was the very heart of the factory, and the beginning of all that happened in it.

Joe Watkins started work in the slaughterhouse in 1952 on his fifteenth birthday. He used to go over the bridge to the Boning Department. 'It was pretty grim work and smelly. I don't know how I stuck it. The people who worked there became your family so that helped.' One of his jobs was taking pituitary glands (pea size) out of pigs' heads with tiny tweezers, putting them in jars and taking them to the laboratory. He moved to the Kitchen Department later where he made pies and canned goods. He stayed seven years at Harris before joining Blackford & Son builders.

Derek Freegard: 'On my way home from school I used to watch the pigs being unloaded, where Sainsbury's car park is now, into the pens for slaughter. The men had electric prods to make them move and the pigs used to scream – not a pleasant sound.'

Geoffrey Lucas started his five-year apprenticeship in the Maintenance Department, aged sixteen, in 1948. Their work consisted of general maintenance, repairing and installing new machinery, pipe work, lift maintenance – anything really. His wife Audrey remembers that he said that he worked with a great bunch of guys and had a few laughs with them, while the boss John Bromham used to walk around just shaking his head. Geoff and a few others were members of Calne Fire Service and Harris's were very good in letting them attend callouts. Geoff was made redundant in 1982 after thirty years' service.

Garry Hunt was three years into his four-year Maintenance Engineering apprenticeship when the factory closed in 1982. 'Harris's found me alternative employment at Avon Tyres, Melksham, to finish off the balance of my time. I started two weeks' later and worked there for thirty-two years until I decided to leave.'

Audrey (Small) Lucas worked for Harris before starting a family.

I was an Intrascope Operator, from January 1963 to May 1967, based in the Slaughterhouse. We wore white coats, hairnets and white wellington boots. I remember one person measured two depths of fat on the side of the pig as they came down on a moving bar, and one recorded the figures then we swapped over. The figures were then transferred to the Farmers' Reports when we got back to the office.

Mike Wiggins started work in 1953 after leaving the Army following National Service in Korea. He was a long-distance lorry driver for twenty-seven years, driving a variety of vehicles all over the UK. His wife Muriel, née Angell, also worked at Harris (1942–55) as a shorthand typist in the Postal Department, Traffic Office and Ledger Department.

Steve Thomas worked his three-month summer breaks from university from 1973 to 1976, one of many students covering workers' holidays.

I worked all over the factory, starting on the sausage floor, mainly loading the sausage machines with meat. I also did overtime in pies and loading the lorries in the evenings. As I got older they entrusted me with more responsible tasks. My favourite job was making black puddings, liver sausage and brawn, where I had to scrape the eye muscles that move the eyeballs from the pig skulls. They are the tastiest part of the animal.

To make the black puddings I had to collect the blood from the slaughterhouse and then mix it in a huge bowl (a metre diameter) with fat and pearl barley and the seasoning mix, which had wonderful aromatic odours, replacing the smell of death. It was then chopped with rotating knives as the mixing bowl revolved. I was working on my own and had a recipe to follow.

One day I hadn't had much sleep and work started early, about 6.30 a.m. It was really important that sodium citrate solution was added to the empty churns before the blood went in (about a pint per churn). On this day, I forgot.

I trolleyed the blood across the bridge and up in the lift, oblivious to the fact that the blood-clotting enzymes were working away in the churns. When I tried to pour the blood out of the churn into the mixer a huge semi-solid blood clot slipped out like a metre-long maroon beached whale. There were no black puddings made that day, and a lot of money was lost. I thought I was going to be sacked, but I was just told off. I never made that mistake again.

In my last year I worked on the night shift as a hygiene worker. A small team of us were responsible for cleaning all the production floors. It was weird working in an empty factory in semi-darkness, sometimes just by torchlight. One of our jobs was to flush out cockroaches from underneath the machines with buckets of water. It was hard work but I really enjoyed that job. The camaraderie was amazing working nights. We had some good laughs.

We swept the dirty water from cleaning the floors down the drains. This water ended up in a catchpit about 500 metres away down by the River Marden. I also did a stint cleaning out the catchpit of all the fat that had built up on the screens. It was the smelliest, dirtiest job I have ever done but we were paid triple time.

Rod Pottow qualified as an electrician after a five-year apprenticeship at Harris in the 1950s, receiving his indentures from Sir John Bodinnar. 'A rare honour for someone so far down

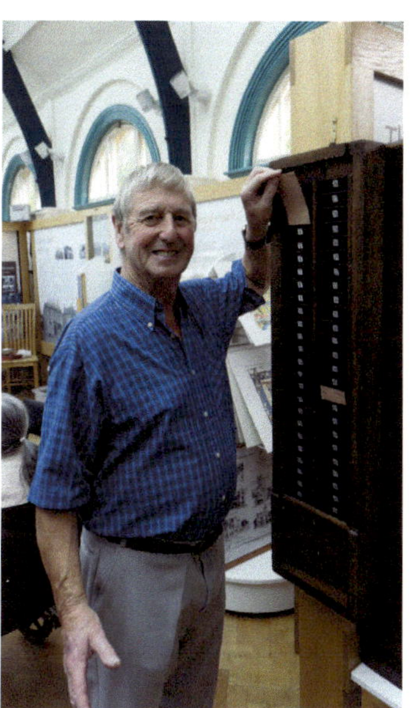

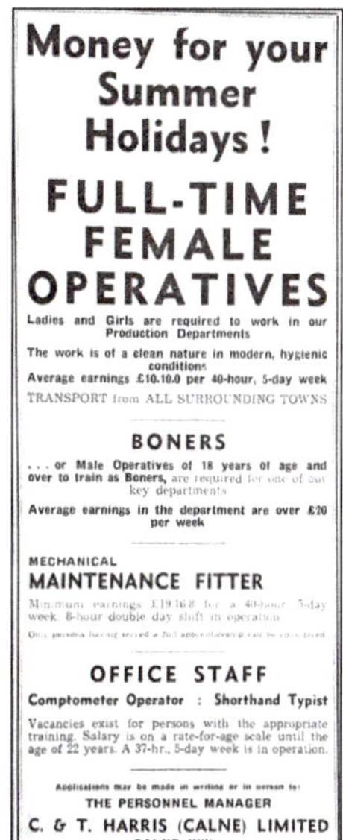

Above left: Former Harris worker Joe Watkins clocks in at Calne Heritage Centre using one of Harris's timecards and clocking in machines at Harris' Reunion Tea Party, 2016. (Author)

Above middle: *Wiltshire Gazette and Herald* advert for summer holiday workers, April 1968.

Above right: Pay packet, Steve Thomas, 1976. His weekly pay before tax is equivalent to £450 today. FMC, the largest meat marketing organisation in Europe, took over the Harris Group in 1962.

the pecking order as me.' In 1964, he married Christine Bull and in 1966, he left to further his career. He retired as Managing Director of Cooper Avon Tyres, Melksham, in 2001.

Christine (Bull) Pottow left school at fifteen and started work in the Postal Department where she learned the location of all the departments. After three months she moved into the Cashiers Department where she worked for thirteen years before leaving to have her family. One of her jobs was to keep a look out for staff going to the bank to collect money for the wages. She remembers having to write down car number plates of vehicles passing by, and working in a special secure room with metal shutters where pay envelopes were filled. 'All pay envelope monies had to balance with the overall total and even if there was a penny difference, no one was allowed to go home.' In 1976, she returned to work part time in the Buying Office. 'I loved my time at Harris's and would have worked there for nothing.'

Karen (Hiscock) Baxter used to work on the bacon slicing line and packing during summer holidays. Her boss, Ted De Boer: 'Wages were very good as were the products. I remember when the inspectors from Marks & Spencer made unannounced visits – it was panic stations. Clean white overalls put on, extra cleaning cloths hastily handed out.'

Kate (Rickell) Jenks was a computer programmer, 1971–75, first based at the Woodlands, moving to new offices over Somerfield supermarket:

I was in the data control office doing the payroll for every branch of the Harris Group. The open-plan layout was a bit of a nightmare for anyone starting new. You'd have to take files to someone across the other side but there was no obvious pathway between all the desks. It might have been modern and forward-thinking but give me nice, regimented rows any day.

The high spot of the week was Friday lunchtime. A couple of people from Harris's shop would come over with reject pies that couldn't be sold in the shop because their pastry crusts were broken. We were allowed to buy them at reduced prices, which we all did – descending on them like seagulls.

Printing Department

Kate's father, Arthur Rickell, was a compositor (1964 to 1982), first in the main building then moving to a single-storey wooden building in Station Road, once used as a wartime community centre. His boss was Jack Kirton and later Tony Grainger. Arthur was on the committee of the Woodlands Club for a long time. He was also a staunch union man and shop steward for the print union The National Graphical Association for many years. In printing unions, the shop steward is also called the FOC – Father of the Chapel. The NGA no longer exists. In 1991, it merged with SOGAT (Society of Graphical and Allied Trades) to form The Graphical, Paper and Media Union.

Mary-Ann (Whale) Angell worked in printing for eight years, starting in 1957 as a printer's assistant on 52 shillings a week; she was later promoted to sales administrator. Her boss was Gerry Ashman, then Jack Kirton.

It was a very busy place, everyone had a particular job to do such as typesetting, proofing, guillotining, knocking up, perforating, jogging, book binding. We did everything from labels, lard liners for boxes, invoices to leather-bound books. The 'Cardboard Girls' also worked here, assembling boxes – creasing and stitching them.

Sheila (Hitchens) Woodman worked in Printing from 1955 to 1961 and is remembered for singing while she worked. One of her jobs was 'jogger':

> We printed lots of invoice books, which needed numbered pages alternating with carbonised sheets and duplicates. We collected sets of loose pages and four of us sat on separate seats, feeding the sheets into the collating machine, which jogged them into order, ready for being glued together in their book covers.

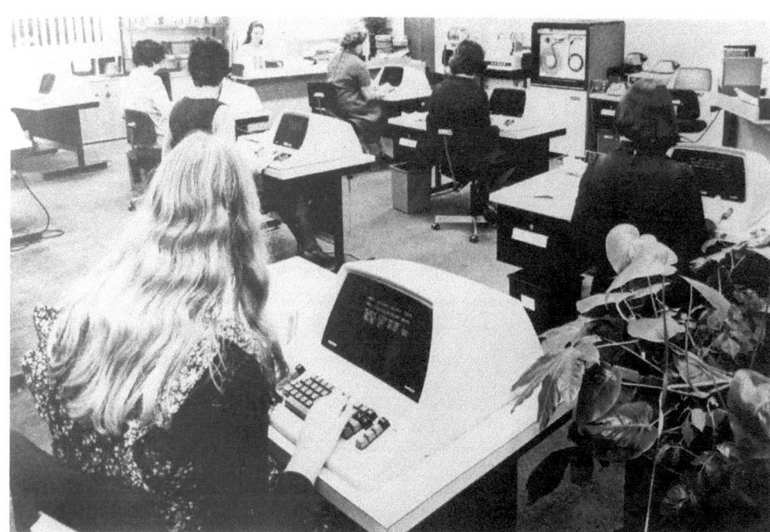

The data entry department in the ADB (Agricultural Database) computer centre, situated above Somerfield, 1976. Information fed into Redifon machines was reproduced on magnetic tape then fed into the computer. FMC Group's first computer was an ICL 1920A, installed in 1972.

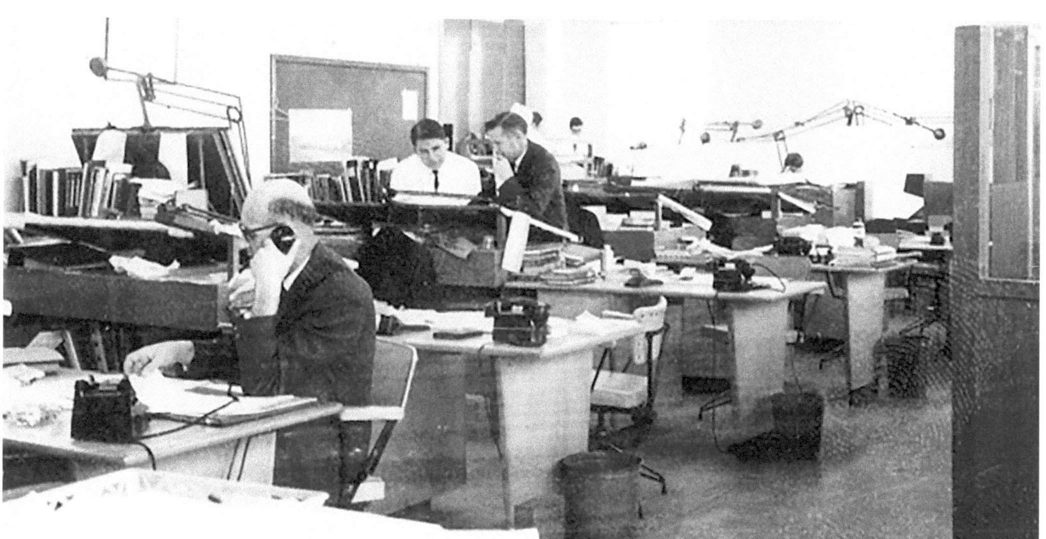

The Drawing Office, 1950s. Ken Holman (on the phone) was an engineering draughtsman, 1951–60, designing machinery for the production line. His father Edward, twenty-five years head gamekeeper at Bowood, packed faggots at Harris for a few years before becoming Calne's first lollipop man. (Susan Waite)

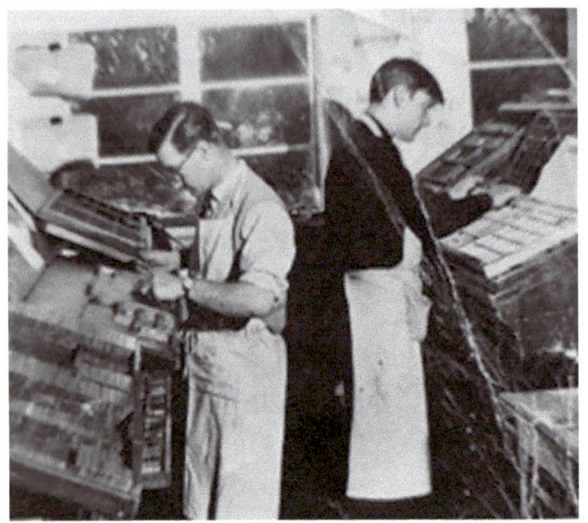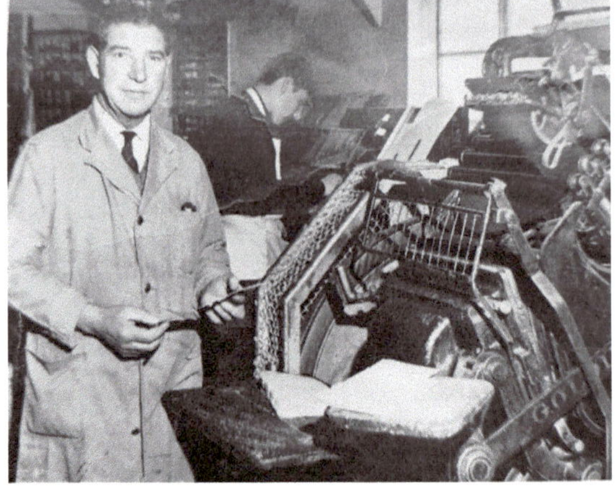

Above left: Printing Department, 1967, Arthur Rickell (left) and Ken Bennett, compositors, Station Road premises.

Above right: Printing Department, 1967. Jack Kirton, supervisor, inspecting the Golding Platen hand-fed machine, bought second hand in 1919 when the department first opened and still used for special jobs.

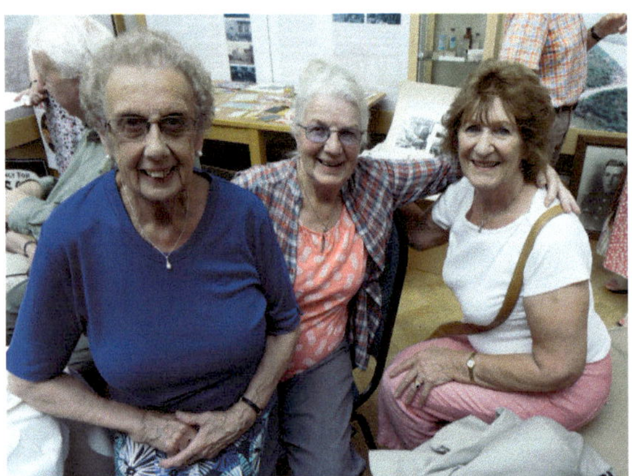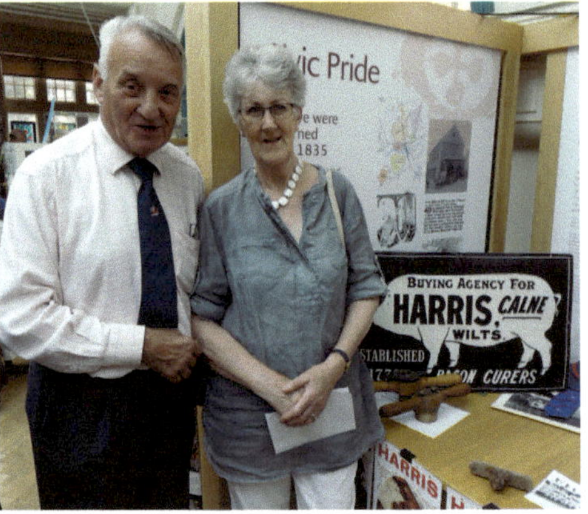

Above left: Printing pals. Left to right: Irene (Haddrell) Haig, Sheila (Hitchens) Woodman and Pauline (Wilkins) Hickman worked together in the Printing Department in the 1950s and 1960s. Harris Tea Party, Calne Heritage Centre, 2016. (Author)

Above right: William 'Bill' Sealy started as a trainee manager in 1962. He was promoted in 1974 to Factory Manager at the Harris/FMC Dunmow Flitch Bacon Factory, Essex. His sister-in-law Barbara Sealy is the daughter of James Smellie, traffic manager from 1935 to 1967. Harris's Tea Party, 2016. (Author)

Harris Retail Shop, No. 13 Church Street.
The shop sold a wide range of factory produce including fresh meat, offal, pigs' feet, pigs' tails and eyepieces, which, according to the memoirs of John Bromham (born in 1909), 'provided a cheap source of protein and fat for working class people'. Also very popular

were 'seconds' (not perfect pies and pasties) sold cheaply. Harris workers received discount cards to use in the shop.

William 'Bill' Ponting, shop manager, started work in 1934 and clocked up fifty years' service, which also included his seven years in the Army during the Second World War.

Derek Phillimore worked there from 1973to 1980 and remembers George Ash, Leslie Grainger, Bill Smith, Frank Lythall, Brenda Smith, and Jean Gale.

Marilyn Somers: 'The shop sold dried pigs' bladders, which you blew up like a balloon, tied with string and then used as footballs. The bladders were more commonly seen full of lard and strung up in the window. Lard was a very popular product used in cooking.'

Simon Bewley: 'I used to buy neckbones, which were cooked very slowly at home all morning on the Rayburn. Nothing tastier, especially with dumplings. I remember the red ham slicing machine, and the big wooden butcher's block being scrubbed clean.'

Clive Seal: 'I loved buying a big slice of the square egg and pork pie [Gala] with just the right amount of jelly under the perfect pastry. With a scrape of mustard and some salad, lovely.'

Medical Centre

Opened in April 1969, it operated twenty-four hours a day. Sister J. H. Arthur, very experienced in industrial health, was in charge. Apart from dealing with all injuries and illnesses of 1,500 workers, they did routine health examinations of staff employed in food handling, and periodic check-ups of executives and managerial staff. A local GP visited once a week, and was also available for emergencies; one of his partners was always available 24/7.

Richard King: 'I had to visit there for a medical when I started at Harris, aged fifteen. To get there, I had to go through the Typing Pool where all the women whistled and catcalled at me. What an introduction to my working life!'

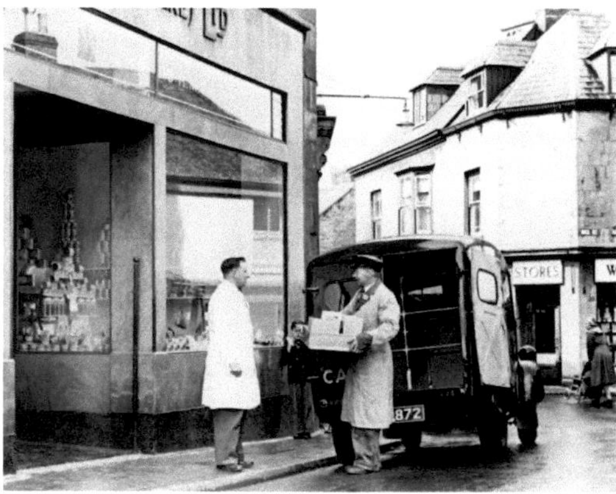

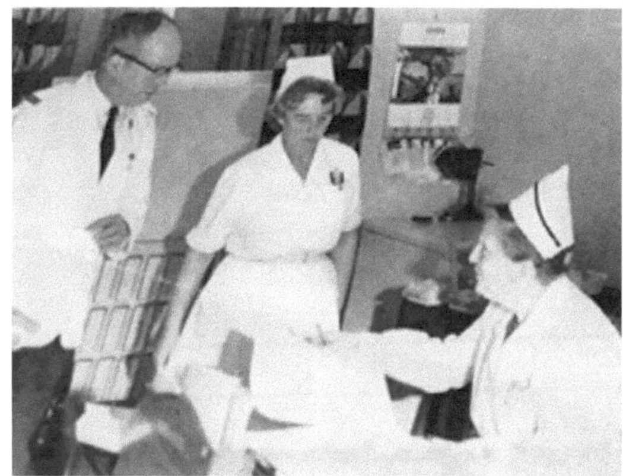

Above left: Harris Retail Shop, No. 13 Church Street, 1960s. Shop manager William 'Bill' Ponting is in the white coat. The row of buildings, owned by Harris, were re-faced after the Second World War, in a neo-Georgian style. Now The Wellbeing Clinic.

Above right: Medical Centre Office, c. 1970. Sister J. H. Arthur at her desk with Mr George Phelps, SEN, and Nursing Auxiliary, Mrs T. Lewis.

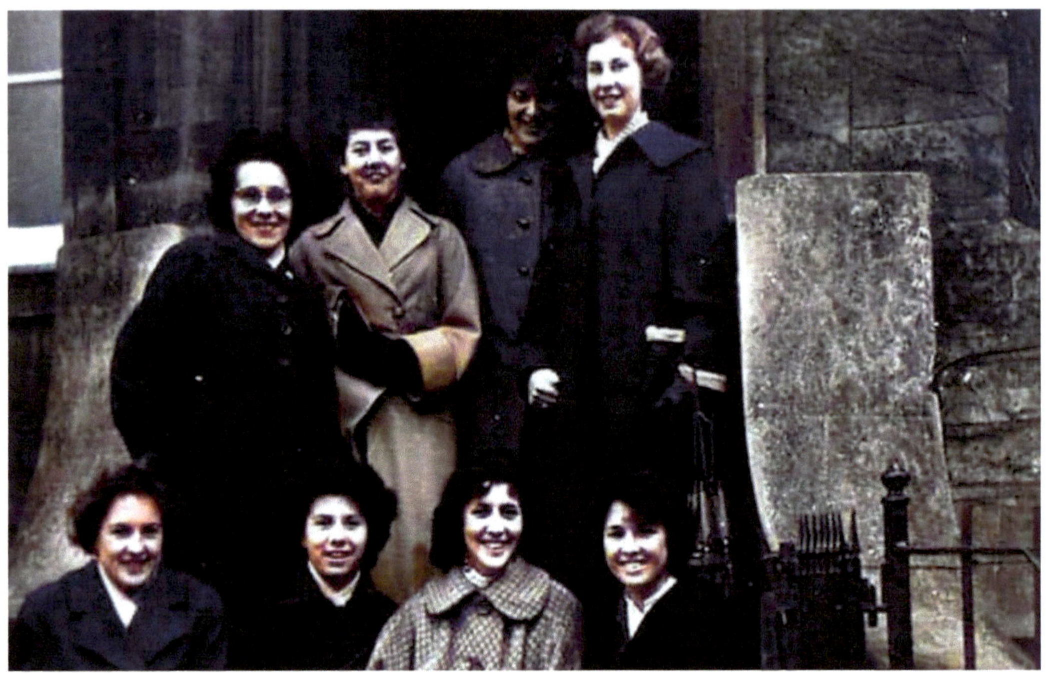

Staff of Sales Ledger Department outside Bank House, 1958. Back left to right: Vera Lugg, Jean Ponting, Yvonne Brewer and Ann Gunning. Front left to right: Janet Cleverly, Shirley Rose, Marlene Brewer and Jenny Hooper. (Dave Edwards)

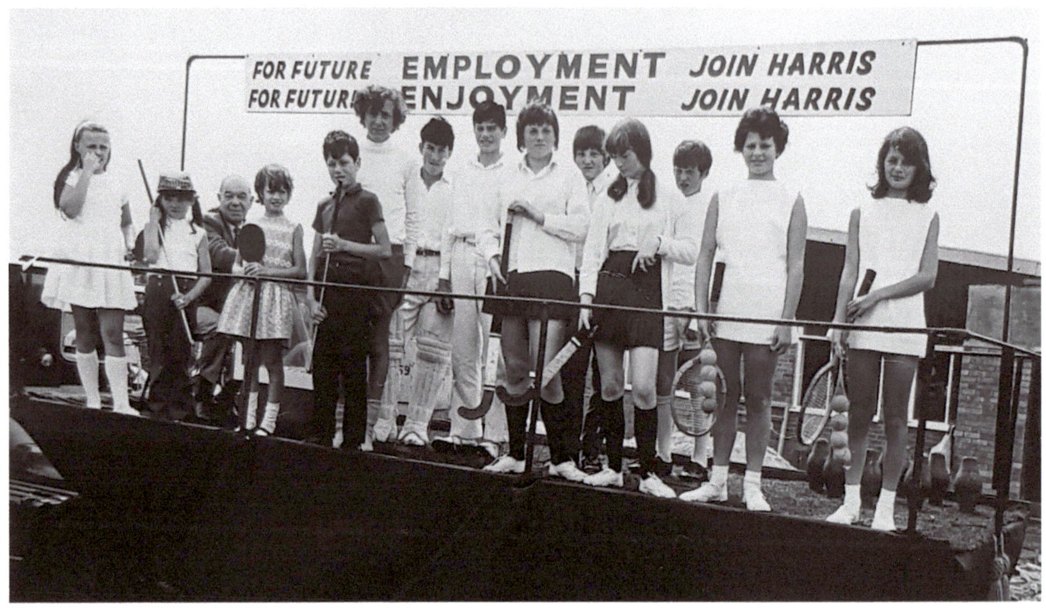

Carnival float, *c.* 1970. Children of Harris workers representing 'The Sporting World' and promoting future employment at Harris's. Percy Carter (seated), Pie Department foreman, received a gold watch for fifty years' service in 1971. He was made redundant in 1982. (Julie (Godwin) Edwards)

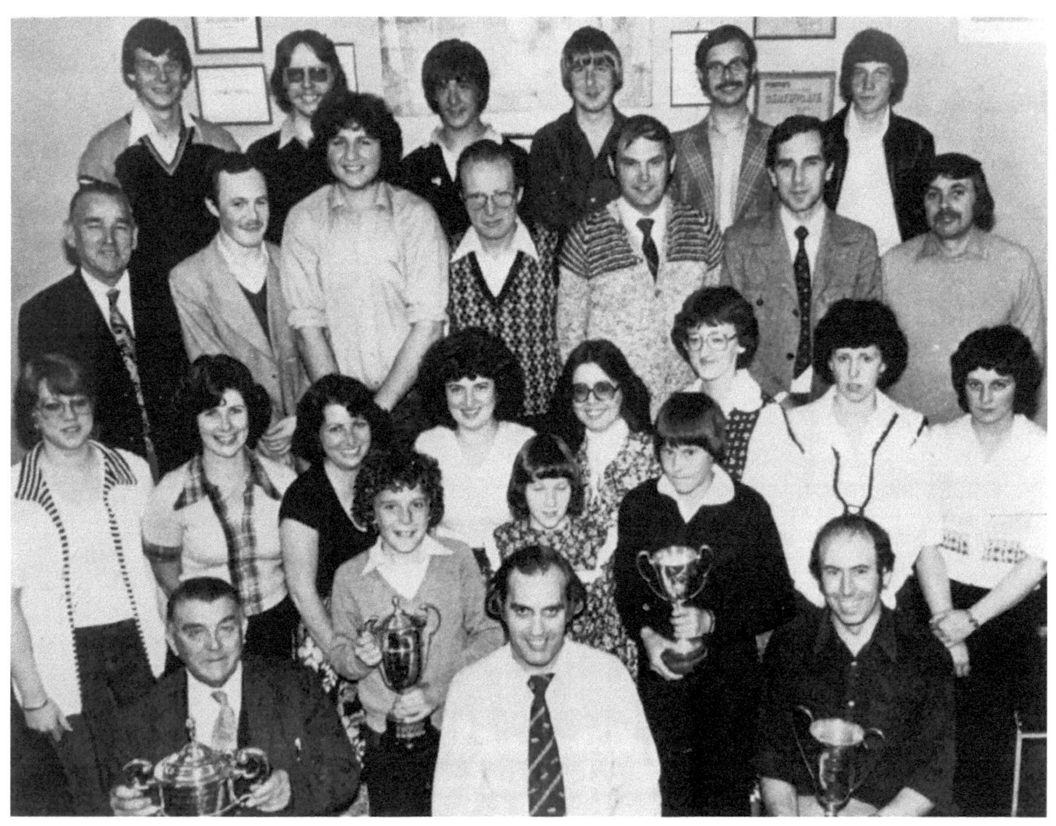

West of England brass band champions, Harris Silver Band, 1980. Formed in 1925 as Calne Silver Band, they were sponsored by Harris in 1978–83. Conductor Mervyn Styles is front centre. Trophies are held (left to right) by Bill Goodship, Chris Downham, Annette Summers and Godfrey Slade.

Joy Allenross: 'I remember going to the Medical Centre when l cut the top off my finger using the cutting machine in the Postal Department. I've still got the scar from fifty years ago.'

Sally Robertson: 'I used to work in the Pie Room on the mini pork pies line squishing the meat down and putting on the pastry lids. I had an upset stomach one time and had to give a stool sample [sent to the Laboratory for testing]. I was moved to Canning where I couldn't pass on any germs.'

Les Fish worked in Boning: 'I paid them quite a few visits – usually cuts to the hand from the knives.'

Michael Bracken was also a regular visitor: 'I wasn't very good at boning a joint or a side of bacon. If you had a slight scratch and it touched a bone, it could become infected.'

Audrey Lucas remembers queuing for Dr Pctcr Rivett to give her a flu jab. 'I fell down some stairs once and had to go there every day and sit with my arm in iced water for a while till the bruise came out.'

9
Closure and Demolition, 1982–86

'If we cannot produce sausages and bacon in Wiltshire, it is a sad day for Britain.'
Richard Needham, MP for North Wiltshire, *Hansard*, 13 February1980

A gradual build-up of events brought about the closure of C. & T. Harris: foot and mouth (1973), recessions (1973–75) and economic stagnation and high unemployment (1979–82). Sales were affected by competition from the Danish bacon industry, along with a change in public taste towards a sweeter cure.

One of biggest blows came with the loss of Marks and Spencer's contract, which accounted for 30 per cent of their total production. In addition, North Wiltshire MP Richard Needham blamed FMC's 'indifferent management which had constantly changed and inadequate capital investment as the main reason for closure'.

Gazette & Herald's front-page headline for 22 April 1982 was 'Harris to be axed but it's no surprise'. Graham Tanner reported:

> Since Britain entered the Common Market, trading has become increasingly difficult due to the weighing of the money scales in favour of the Danes, the Dutch and the Irish. The position became so acute some months before the redundancies of April 1980 were announced, Harris's sacked around forty of its slaughtermen just as the slaughterhouse had been upgraded to meet EEC standards, at a cost of £400,000 [in the region of £1,727,000 today] much of which came from EEC funds; the new facilities were never used.

Local builder Ken Hulbert remembers: 'It was a huge undertaking – many men and many months of work upgrading the lairage, and old slaughterhouse, parts of which were in a dreadful state –pretty gruesome.' While excavating for a new lift shaft, they found wooden stakes and ancient steelwork from the original construction, possibly as early as 1800. 'I knew then that the place was destined to close. It was just not big enough. Not viable. They had already cut back on pigs and were buying in carcases.'

The closing down of Harris was front page news in the *Gazette & Herald* for several months. Peter Clark, General Manager, was greeted by hissing and booing from staff when the factory closure was announced at a meeting at Woodlands Social Club. Andy Brewer, of the Pie Department, told the *Gazette* reporter, 'We thought this would happen. You could see it coming. Trade was going down and the place was generally deteriorating. I think Calne will become a ghost town.'

The factory doors closed on 15 July 1982. 1,300 people still worked there, 400 of which took early retirement or redundancy. FMC was acquired by Hillsdown Holdings in 1983.

Shortly after its closure, the contents – from cutlery and curtains to typewriters and Chubb safes – were sold by auction on 23 September 1982, held on site by auctioneers Tilley & Noad. Transport and Distribution Manager John Godwin, who was left sole representative for FMC, supervised the movement of equipment and fittings from the buildings. Homes were found for major items such as gas boilers, which were acquired by British Steel.

It was rumoured that Asda was interested in the site. However, North Wiltshire District Council (NWDC) bought the 6-acre site, including Harris properties in Church Street; the site was secured until demolition began on 14 May 1984. The first blow of the wrecking ball by T. W. Robinson, Demolition, Ponytpool, was watched by Mayor Cllr Edna Syms and Michael Flintoff, Chairman of NWDC, and crowds of local people and TV reporters.

After the demolition, the town centre landscape changed completely, opening up views such as St Mary's Church tower, which could now be seen from every direction. The Pippin side of the River Marden was grassed over, creating a green area in the town centre. The sites remained undeveloped for a long time – a very long time.

Tilley & Noad notice, sale of contents of Harris Factory, 23 September 1982. Former Calne Mayor David Lock was in charge of the sale. *Gazette and Herald* headline reported: 'Giant pie ovens fetch only £5 each at auction.'

C. & T. HARRIS (CALNE) LIMITED

AUCTION SALE

Thursday 23rd September 1982

FACTORY No. 1 (commences at 10 a.m.)

GROUND FLOOR Lots 1 - 245 Processing Machinery, Stainless Steel Tables, etc. (Rooms 1 & 2). Lots 246 - 249 (Transport Office) 250 - 336 (Loading Bay) 280 - 315 and 337 - 353 (Chill Room) 335 Elevator (Dixons Yard)

FIRST FLOOR Lots 361 - 476 and 701 - 742 Office Furniture, Tables, Chairs, Desks, Filing Cabinets etc. in Room 1. 482 - 488 Cabinets & Lockers in Store Room. 489 - 519 Surgery Equipment 520 - 544 Typist Pool Office Furniture 545 - 585 Canteen Equipment MAIN TYPIST POOL Lots 584A - 605 Typewriters, etc. CHUBB SAFE Lot 625 EXECUTIVE SUITE 626 - 647 Partners Desks and Tables, Chairs, Cabinets, Kitchen Fittings, Electric Lights, Curtains, etc.

RETORT LEVEL 648 - 663 **CELLAR** 665 - 673 **TOP FLOOR** 740 & 741 Timber/Oven
NOTE These last 3 items to be viewed only if accompanied by Authorised Staff.

FACTORY No. 2 (commences at 12-30 p.m.)

Lots 1001 - 1500 **plus** Engineering Equipment, Carpentry Equipment

THE AUCTIONEERS are TILLEY & NOAD and representatives will be available on the View Day Wednesday 22nd September from 10 a.m. to 4.30 p.m. Commissions to Purchase can only be accepted if in writing.

THE CONDITIONS OF SALE ARE AS PRINTED AND DISPLAYED

THE AUCTIONEERS OFFICE is in the FORECOURT of FACTORY No. 1 and will be manned continuously during the Sale and on Friday 24th September from 9 a.m. - 12 noon & 1 p.m. - 4 p.m. No Lot will be delivered without a receipt. **Sales Office Tel. 812261 Wed-Thur-Fri.**

(FOR CONDITIONS OF SALE SEE OVERLEAF)

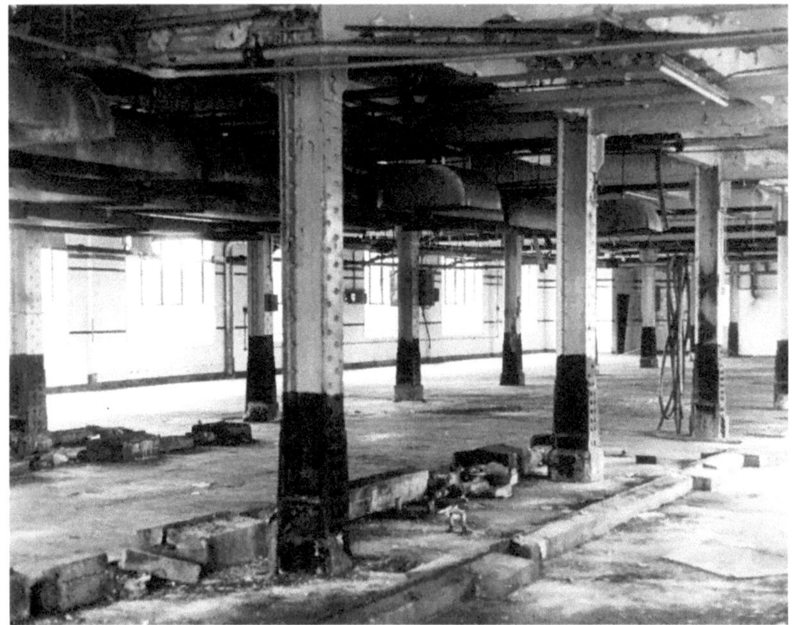

Inside Harris premises after closure, prior to demolition. It gives an idea of the scale of the building and the construction – steel columns with heavy rivets visible.

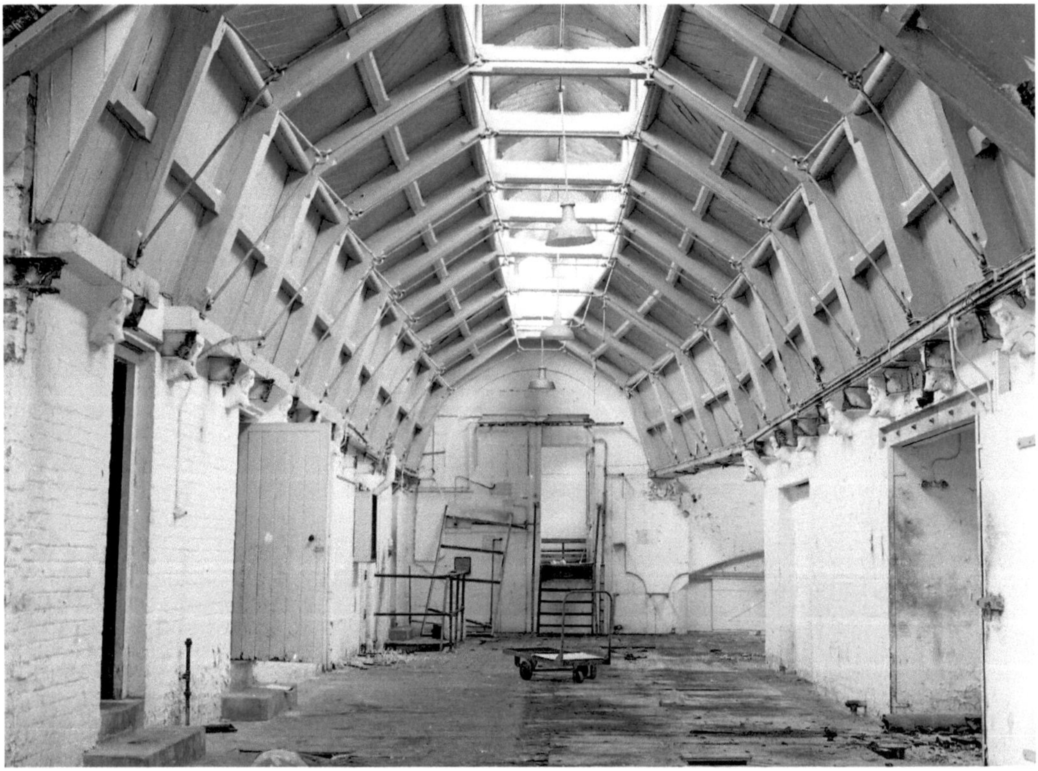

Inside former hanging room of sides of bacon. A high-ceilinged room with roof trusses supported by corbels representing boars' heads alternating with heads of Circe, goddess of corn. Calne Heritage Centre has several of the boar's head corbels on display.

Right: Demolition Day, 14 May 1984. On the left Cllr Michael Flintoff, Chairman of North Wiltshire District Council, with Mayor Cllr Edna Syms, posing with the wrecking ball of T. W. Robinson, Pontypool, and some of the first bricks to fall.

Below: Harris demolition in progress reveals rear of Church Street buildings and St Mary's Church tower, *c.* 1984. It is now the Heritage Quarter car park.

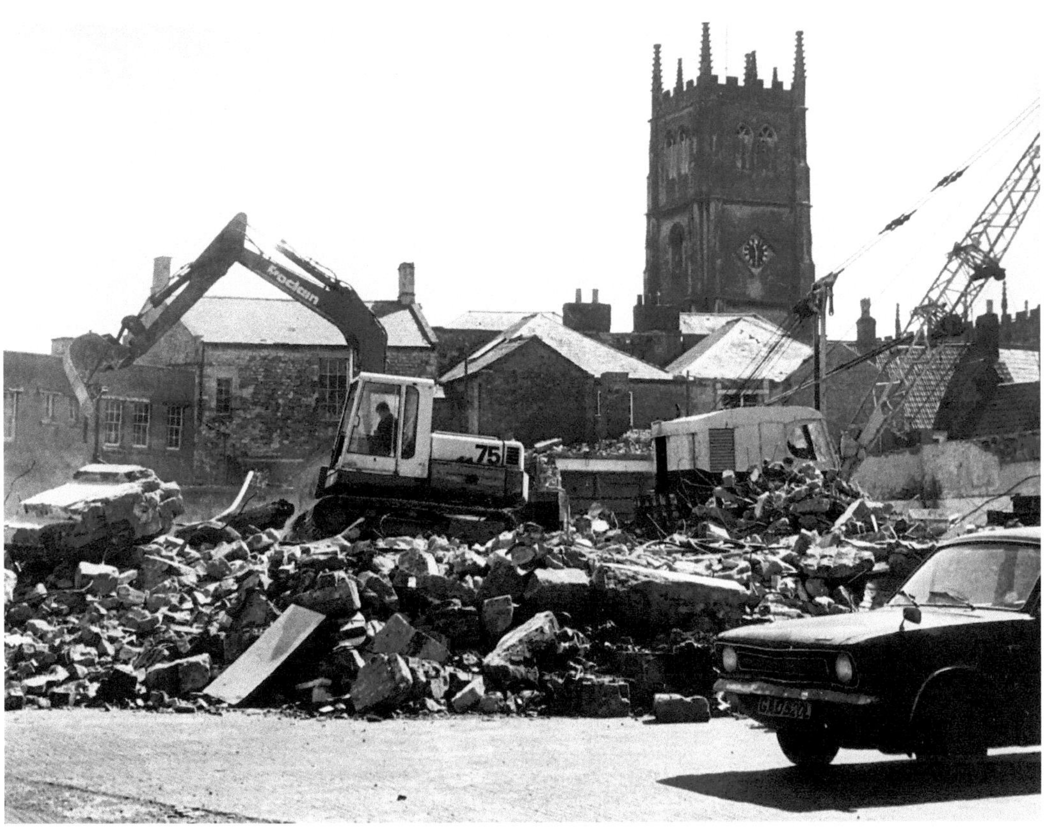

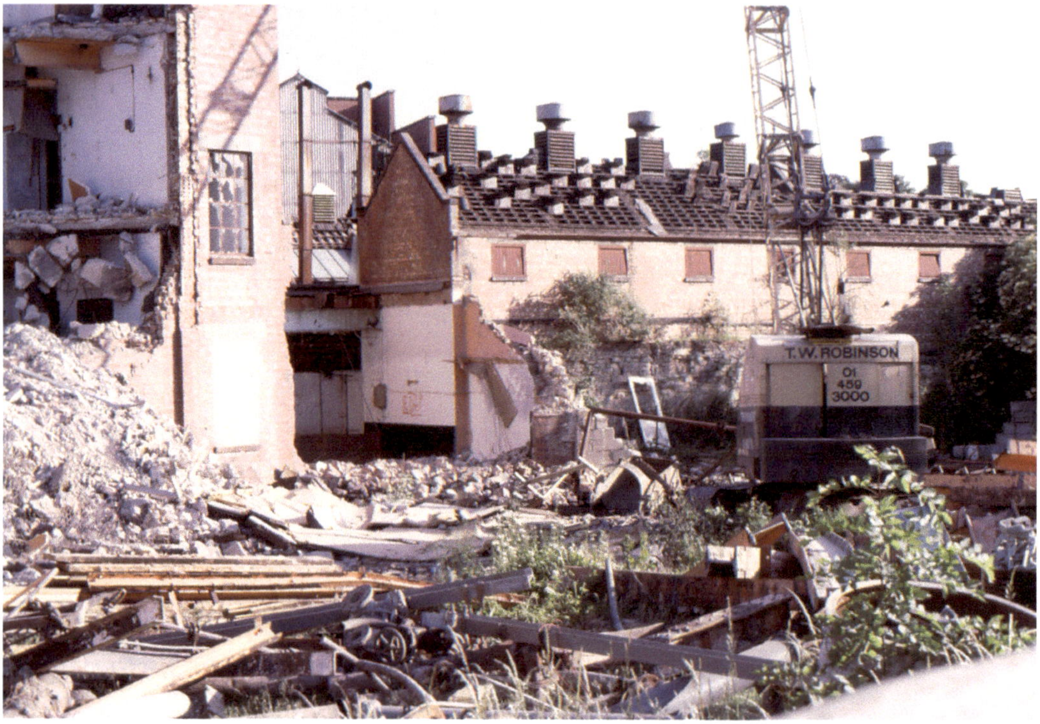

View of vents from the smoke stoves.

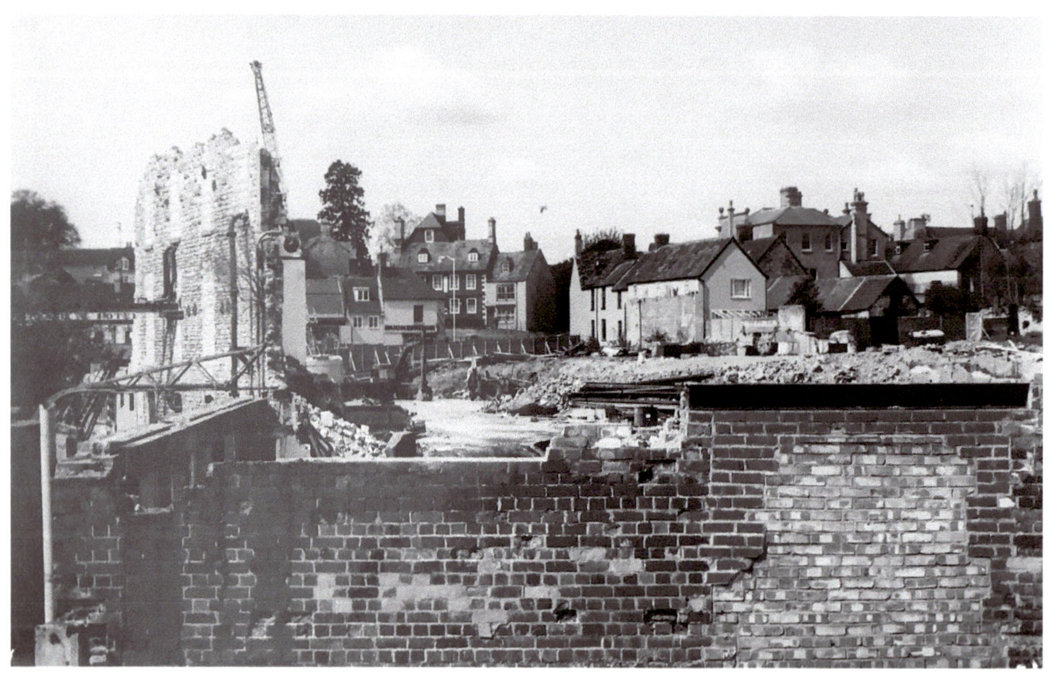

View across demolition site from The Pippin shows Market Hill and Buckeridge's store now
visible.

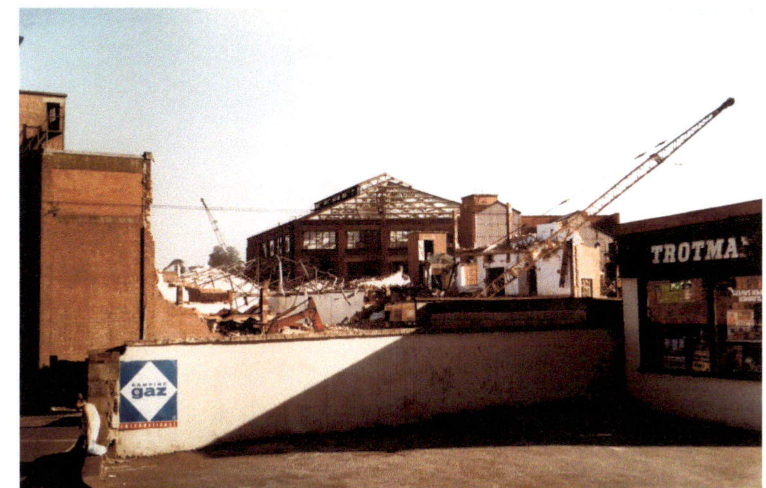

View of the demolition site from Trotman & Sons, ironmongers, The Pippin, 1984/5.

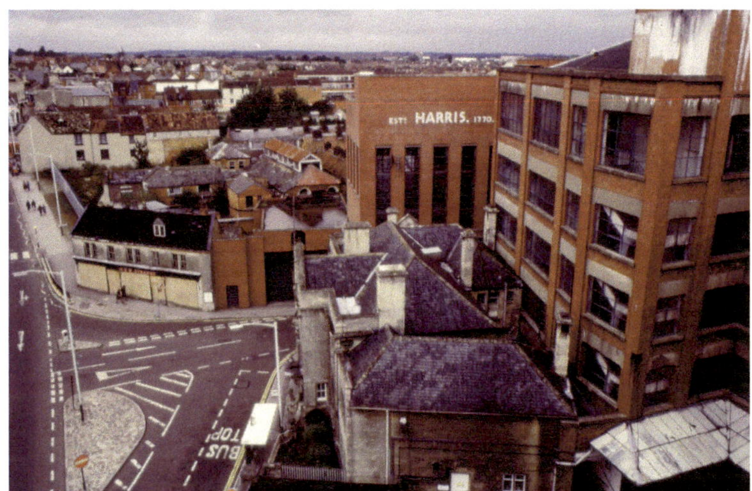

Right: Before demolition, view across the corner of Church Street, Bank House and the huge power station dominating the Pippin side.

Below: View from The Strand of the grassed over Harris site and the Church Street turning, 1990.

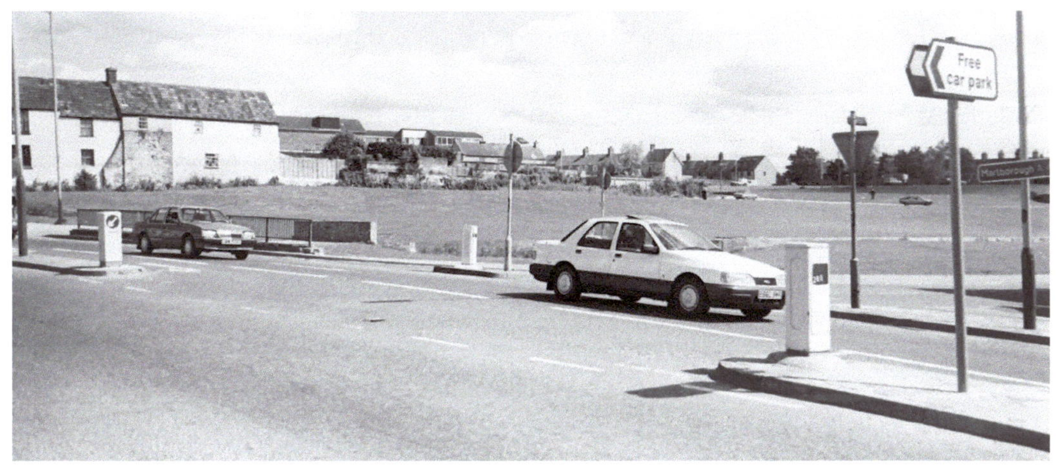

10

Regeneration: The Calne Project, 1986–2008

'Calne plans to make silk purse out of a sow's ear.'

Guardian, 21 March 1988

The Calne Project deserves a whole book of its own, to do justice to the complex subject: the nature of its work, the large number of people involved, the decades of planning, raising money, consultation, and eventual development. There were the twists and turns, the ups and downs and many controversies – political and economics-related – that arose during this period of regeneration of the Harris site.

The Calne Project Development Trust, working title The Calne Project, was set up as an independent charity in 1986:

1 – The Trust is established for the public benefit for the following purposes in the area comprising the Calne Community Area as designated by the North Wiltshire District Council which shall here in after be referred to as 'the Area of Benefit'.
2 – to promote high standards of planning and architecture in or affecting the Area of Benefit.
3 – to secure the preservation protection development and improvement of features of historic or public interest.

Former Calne Town Councillor and Mayor Mike White (1990) was one of five North Wiltshire District Council (NWDC) representatives on The Calne Project Executive Committee, with P. Green, Norman Hills, and former Calne Town Mayors Steve Fairbrass (1980) and Charles Hickling 1984/85.

Other representatives included Wiltshire County Councillors Professor J. Ilersic, Ms J. Mactaggart and Robert Syms, now Sir Robert, Conservative MP for Poole; Calne Town Councillors Peter Treloar and Don Wiffen; Jane Macpherson, Calne Civic Society; Mrs F. Martin, Calne & District Business Association; Ray Downham, Calne Community Council; and representatives from English Heritage.

The Earl of Shelburne was President and Gordon Michell, Director, having successfully overseen the regeneration of the former lead-mining town of Wirksworth in Derbyshire.

Mike White became Vice-chairman in 1993. He looks back at that time:

Nineteen years elapsed between the closure of the Harris business, the demolition of its factory buildings and the eventual redevelopment of its sites on either side of the River Marden in the town centre. Years that saw conflict between NWDC and the townspeople of Calne, represented by The Calne Project, its District Councillor members, other civic groups and individuals. That conflict was resolved but then a national economic downturn had a serious impact on the proposals that were brought forward for the main Bank Site between Church Street and the A4. This led to a frustrating period that culminated in more conflict with NWDC and within The Project itself. The resolution of that conflict led to the eventual development of both sites.

Along the way, national politicians and royalty supported the Project. Lord Jenkin of Roding, Secretary of State for the Environment, visited in 1985 and 1988; and Paddy Ashdown, leader of the Liberal Democrats, visited in 1989. Prince Charles was invited by the Project and visited on 25 March 1988 to open the newly converted Marden House (former Harris records store) on the Wharf. Afterwards, he visited Colemans Farm to inspect environmental improvement works to Woodruffe Square by NWDC.

When the Queen came to open the new library on 7 December 2001, Calne people, who had lost so much and suffered for so long, felt that they mattered after all. The town that many called 'a dump', not helped by English China Clays (ECC) waste site on the town's northern outskirts, could breathe a sigh of relief as it regained its sense of self-respect.

The completion of Phase 1 (Bank Side) included restoration work on listed buildings by Wiltshire Historic Buildings Trust with financial support from English Heritage, and new housing in Church Street, the building of Carnegie Mews, and public car park. The council decided to undertake the final phase of the project, and architects Aaron Evans Associates (Bath), who had been awarded the original contract, were commissioned to design a new library, retail units and flats on the west side; this also involved the diversion of the Marden through the town centre. The architects received the award for 'Best practice in regeneration' from the British Urban Regeneration Association (BURA) 2004.

Sue Boddington, former Calne librarian, played an important role in the work:

I was involved in planning the new library, and once we were up and running, I filled in the application to the Royal Institute of Architects (RIBA) to put the building up for an architectural prize. We won 'Best small public building' Award. When we opened in July 2001, people were queuing all along The Strand to get in. We issued 1,000 books in the first hour. Some people were not impressed with the design and called it 'the gasometer', while others thought the height of it was a waste of space and there should have been a second floor.

For several more years, the focus was on Castlefields Development. With the Project job done, the charity was deregistered in 2008.

Calne did not get its day hospital – an extension to Broken Cross Health Centre was planned, or a northern relief road. It did gain a Sainsbury's store, which opened in January 1998, on the site of the old Harris slaughterhouses and piggeries on The Pippin, and Marden House Centre, and the Wharf sheltered housing. In addition, Calne Heritage Centre was officially opened in 2004 by the Earl of Kerry in the old Carnegie Library. This building had always been dwarfed by its neighbour, No. 1 Factory, but was now able to stand proudly on its own.

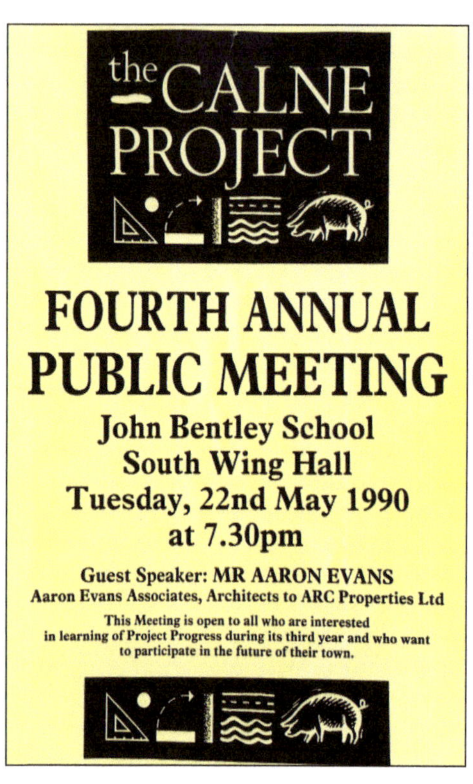

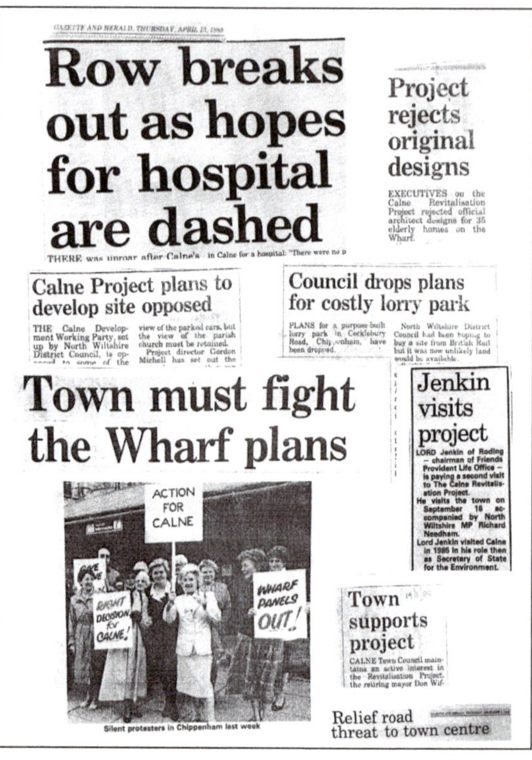

Above left: Poster for The Calne Project Fourth Annual Public Meeting with architect Aaron Evans as a guest speaker, 22 May, 1990.

Above right: Calne Project headlines from the *Gazette and Herald*, 1988/89. The 'Action for Calne' women were protesting about a proposal to use factory-made metal panels on the third-storey parts of the sheltered housing scheme on the Wharf.

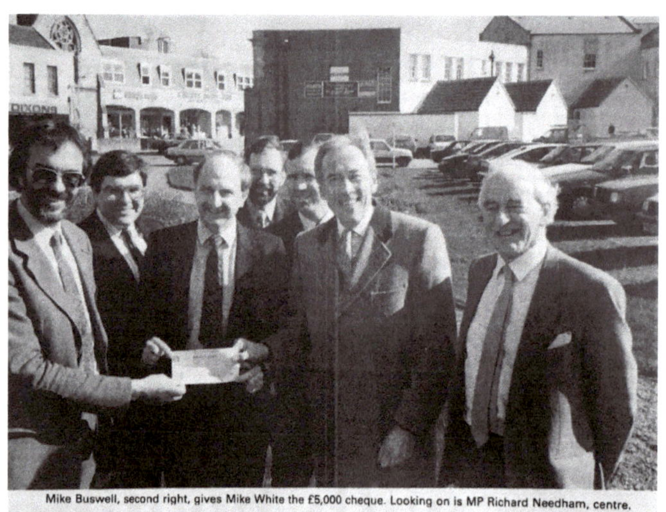

Calne Project Vice-chairman, Mike White, receives a cheque from Mike Buswell, Director Hillsdown Holdings, which took over FMC. North Wiltshire MP Richard Needham, holding the cheque, and Gordon Michell, Director (right). The money boosted funds after English Heritage reduced its financial backing to the project.

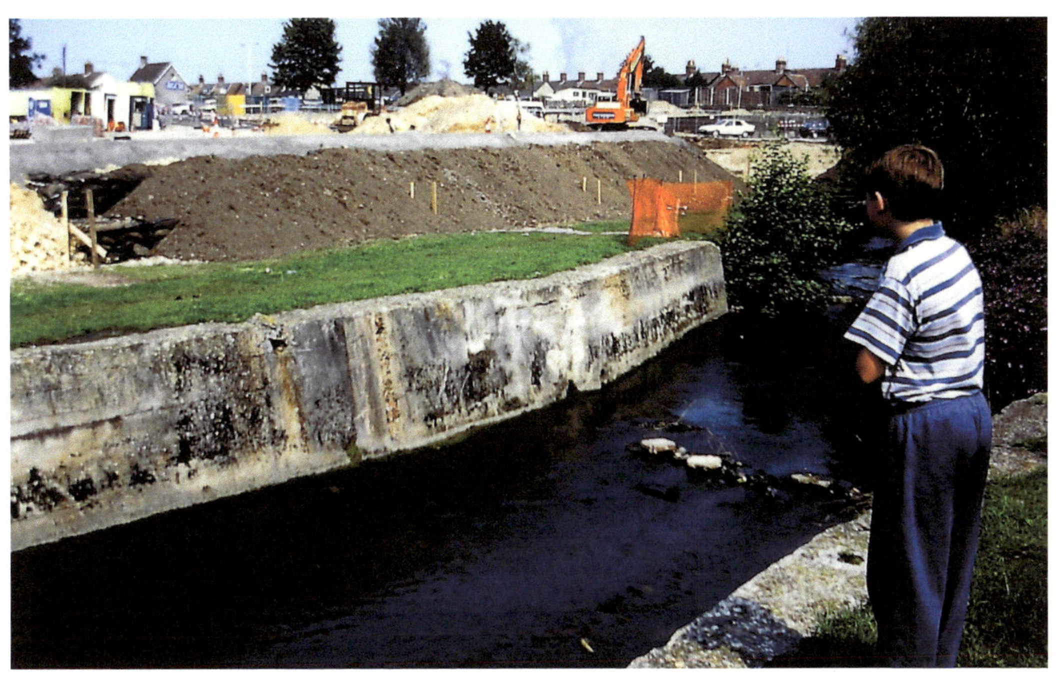

Work beginning on Phase 2 development site for the new library, redirection of the River Marden and Sainsbury's store. (Michael Thomas)

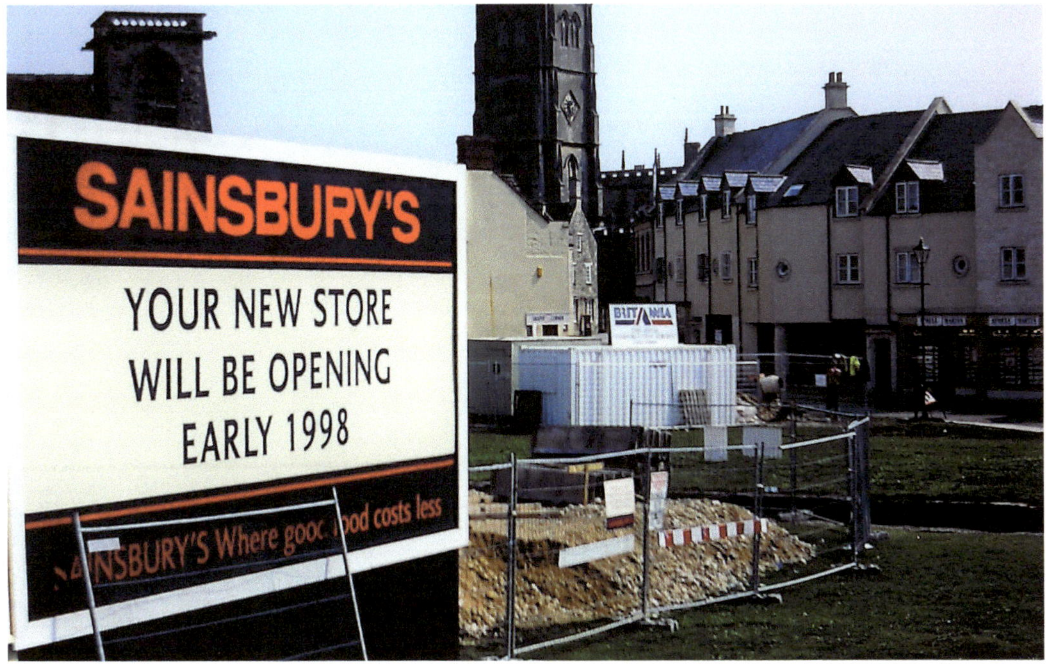

A Sainsbury's store was opened on 27 January 1998 by Lord Sainsbury of Turville. The store manager was Bob Upshall and the number of staff totalled 205 (185 new jobs). The sales area is 15,167 sq. ft (1,409 sq. m). The car park has 254 spaces. (Michael Thomas)

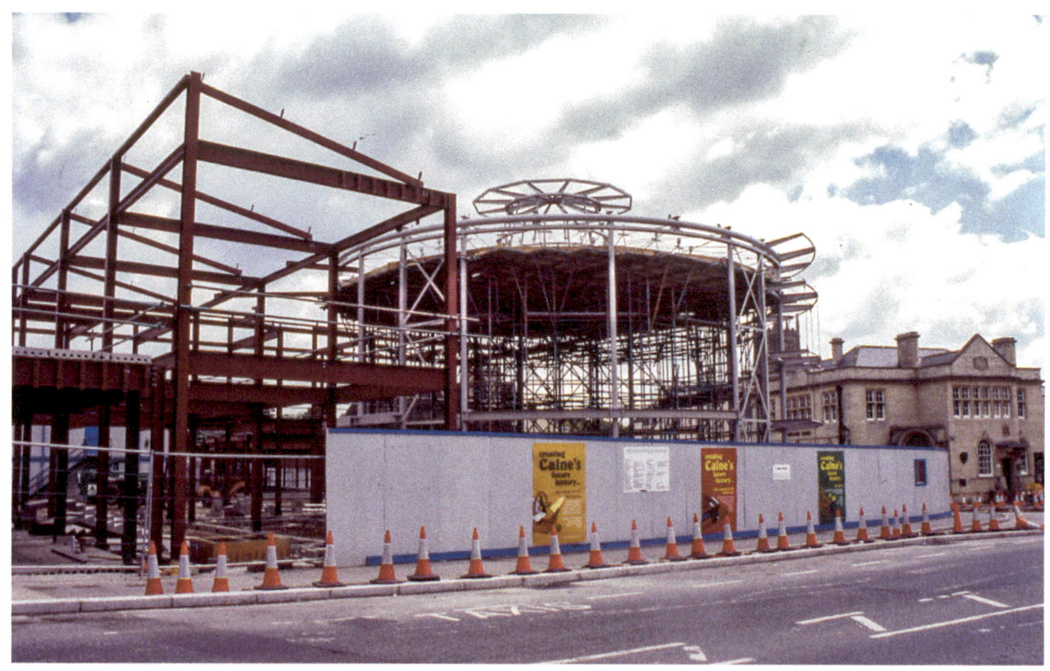

'Creating Calne's future history' posters announce on the boarding around the library under construction. The Strand, July 2000. (Eddy Lane)

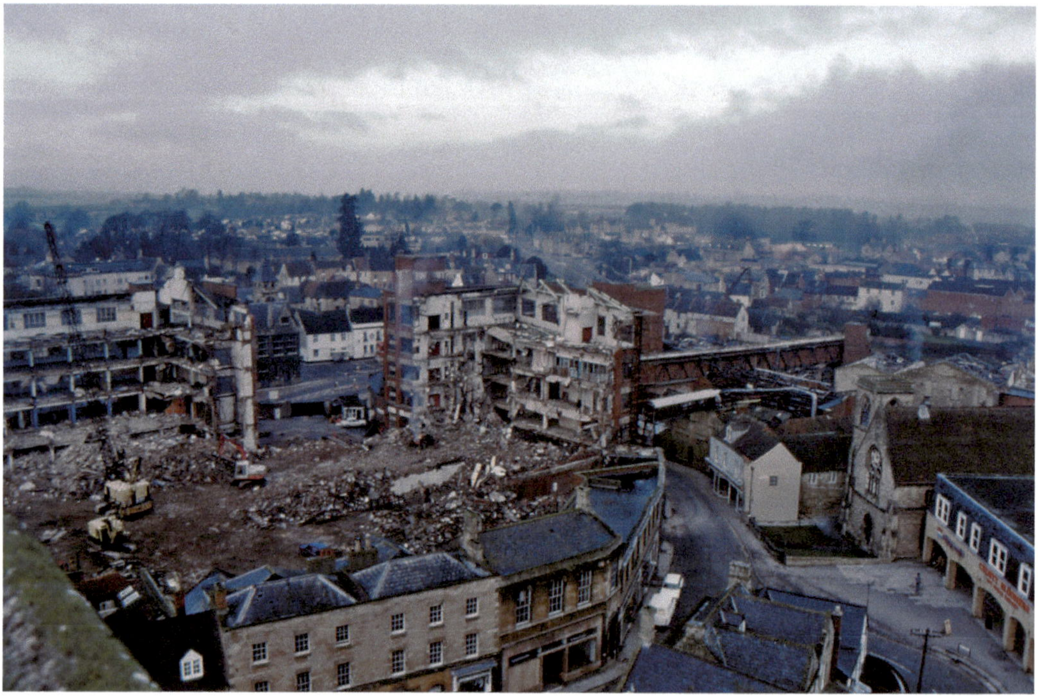

View across Church Street from St Mary's Church tower. Demolition of No. 1 and No. 2 Factories is nearly completed, 1984/85.

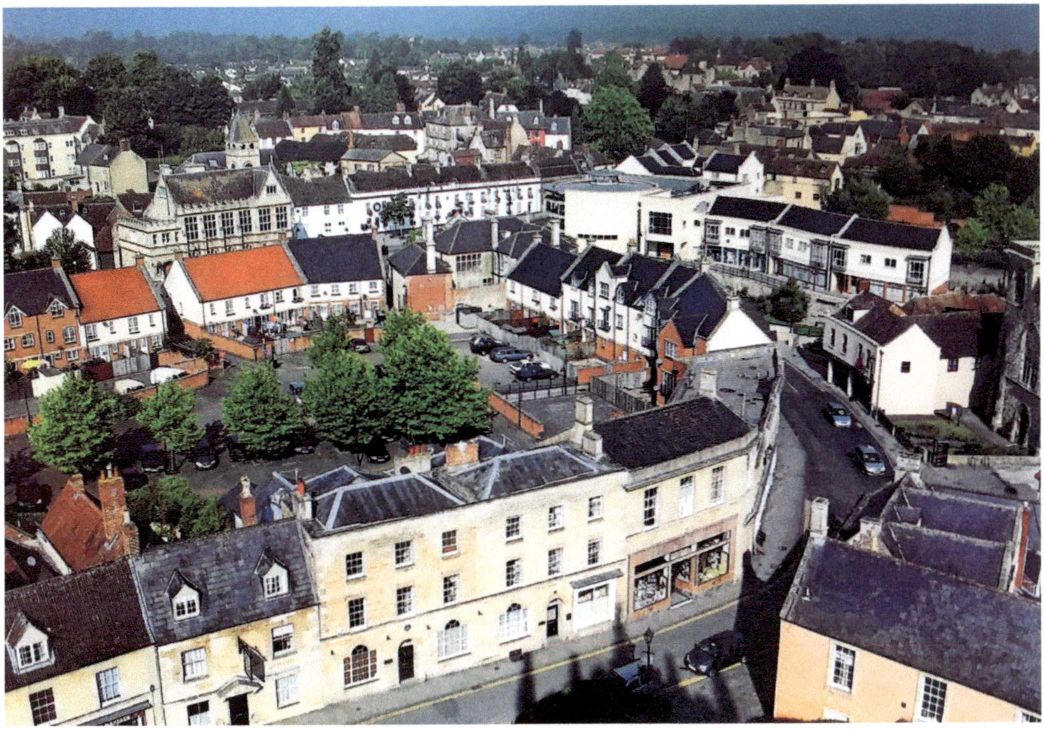

View from St Mary's Church tower of Church Street shows the development of the Harris site. Housing in Bank Row and Carnegie Mews (facing New Road) opened in 1995.

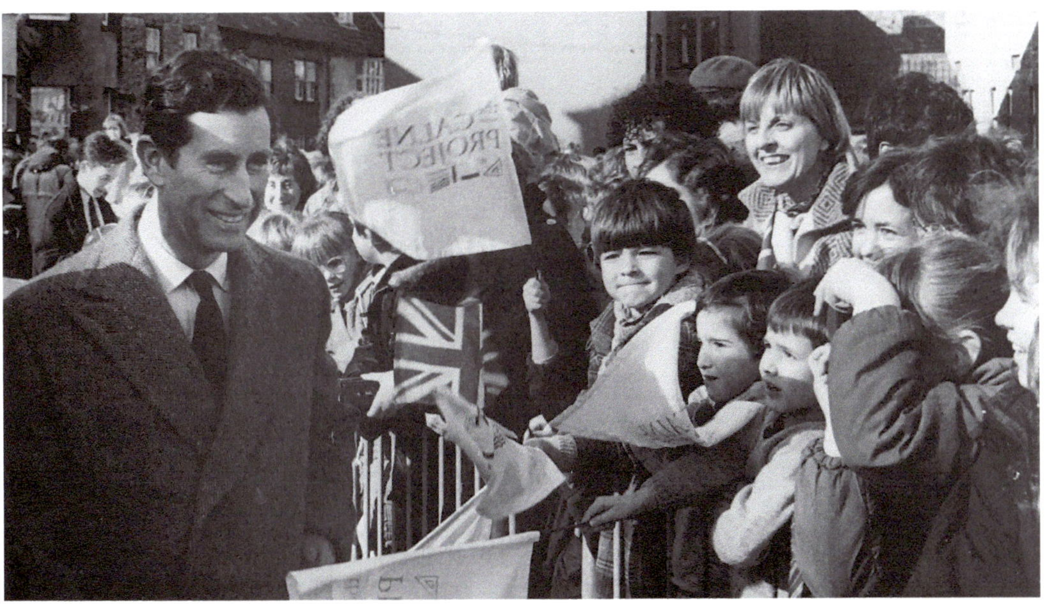

The Prince of Wales visited Calne in 25 March 1988, greeted by schoolchildren at the Wharf where he unveiled a plaque commemorating The Calne Project and the start of work on Marden House Centre.

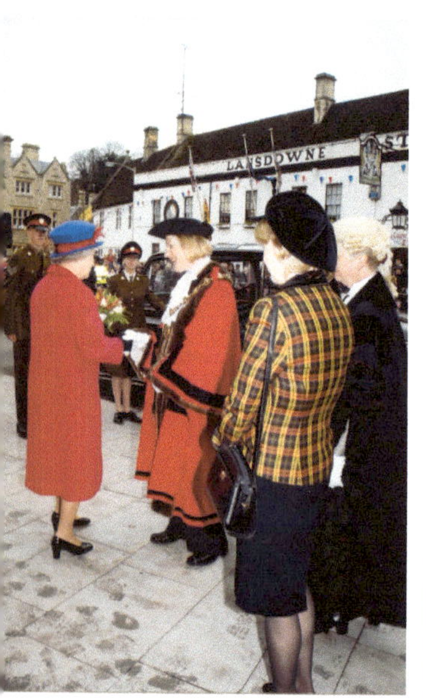
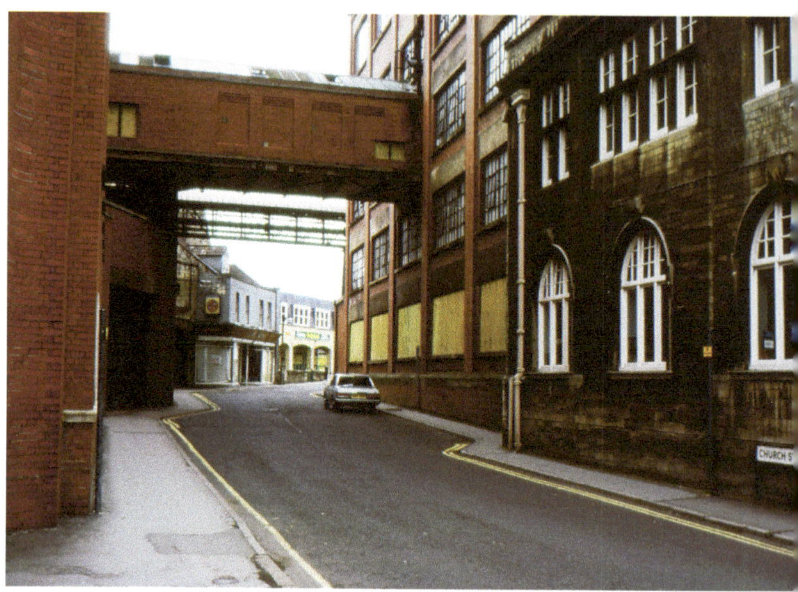

Above left: HRH Queen Elizabeth II visited Calne to open the new library on 7 December 2001. Greeted by Mayor Cllr Elizabeth Watkins and Lt-General Sir Maurice Johnston, Lord Lieutenant of Wiltshire (left).

Above right: Church Street *c.*1980, Leah (Witcomb) Alday remembers: 'I dreaded walking along that part of Church Street under the bridge. The sound of squealing pigs and clattering hooves. Worst of all, the smell – the sinister, bloody smell that hung in the air.'

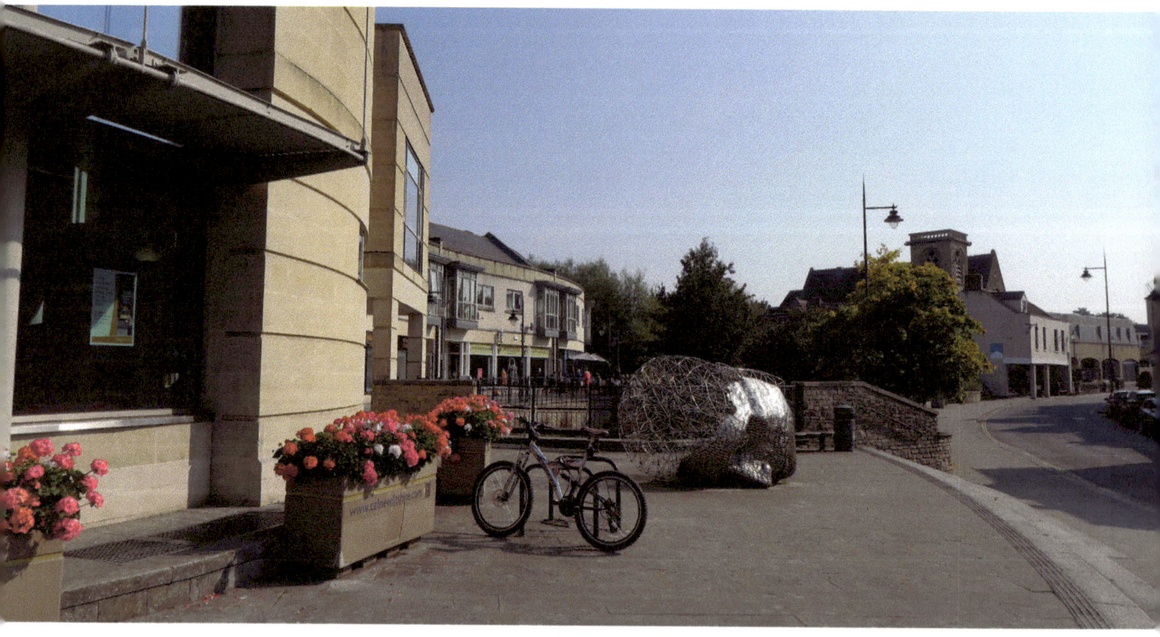

View of Church Street, Library, *The Head* sculpture by Rick Kirby, and Beach Terrace development of Harris's site, 2020. (Author)

11

The Harris Legacy

'Surplus wealth is a sacred trust which its possessor is bound to administer in his lifetime for the good of the community.'

Andrew Carnegie

The imprint of the Harris family can be found all over the town. They contributed to civic life as councillors, mayors, JPs, local and county Board members – making decisions about issues affecting Calne residents. Their power, influence and generosity left the town a richer place with public buildings and spaces they helped to create.

Calne Free Church, 1867–68
Grade II listed.
Charles, Thomas and George Harris were among the principal founders, having broken away from the parish church of St Mary the Virgin. They contributed £250 each towards the £5,000 cost (equivalent to £563,500 today). The church is a registered charity, appearing under its official name 'The Thomas Harris Trust'.

The Town Hall, 1884–86
Grade II listed.
'Franco-Flemish Victorian Gothic' style, it was built on the site of the old town mill. The architect, Bryan Oliver, won a competition to design the building. It was paid for by public subscription and generous donations from the Lansdowne and Harris families. It cost £9,375 (equivalent to £1,147,000 today). The Town Hall complex once housed the town's fire, ambulance and police station.

Thomas Harris purchased land in Church Street on which he built:

The Constitutional Club, 31 Church Street, *c.* 1880
Calne Conservative Club, now flats.

Nos 1–3 Kerry Crescent, New Road, *c.* 1885–99
Grade II listed terrace of three houses 'Free Tudor and Jacobean Revival style', built for his daughters. Now Heritage B&B, a dental practice and private residence.

Ivy Walk, 1887
Gifted 'a roadway for pedestrian traffic from The Green and adjacent parts to the Railway Station'.

The Pavilion and Recreation Ground, Anchor Fields, 1891
A letter from the Mayor Thomas Edward Redman to Thomas Harris Esq. 21 August 1891:

Our warmest thanks for the Recreation Ground with handsome Pavilion and Caretaker's Lodge, which you have so munificently provided for the Town, and which you have today publicly handed over to us, as the Sanitary Authority of the Borough.
  The ground is so conveniently and pleasantly situated and it has been so well laid out and adapted in every way to meet the requirements of those seeking health, recreation, and enjoyment, that it cannot fail to give pleasure to large numbers of people, and we are satisfied it will prove a great boon to the Town and Neighbourhood.

The Conacher Organ, Church of St Mary the Virgin, 1908
The Harris family donated £2,000 (equivalent to £242,000 today) to the church for a new organ by master organ builder Peter Conacher of Huddersfield. The organ case, described by Pevsner as 'very large and sumptuous', was designed by C. R. Ashbee, a leading figure in the Arts and Crafts movement and founder of the Campden Guild.

Calne Free Library, 1905, now Calne Heritage Centre
This was one of 660 Carnegie Libraries in Britain financed by American multimillionaire and philanthropist Andrew Carnegie. He gave £1,200 (£146,870 today) on condition

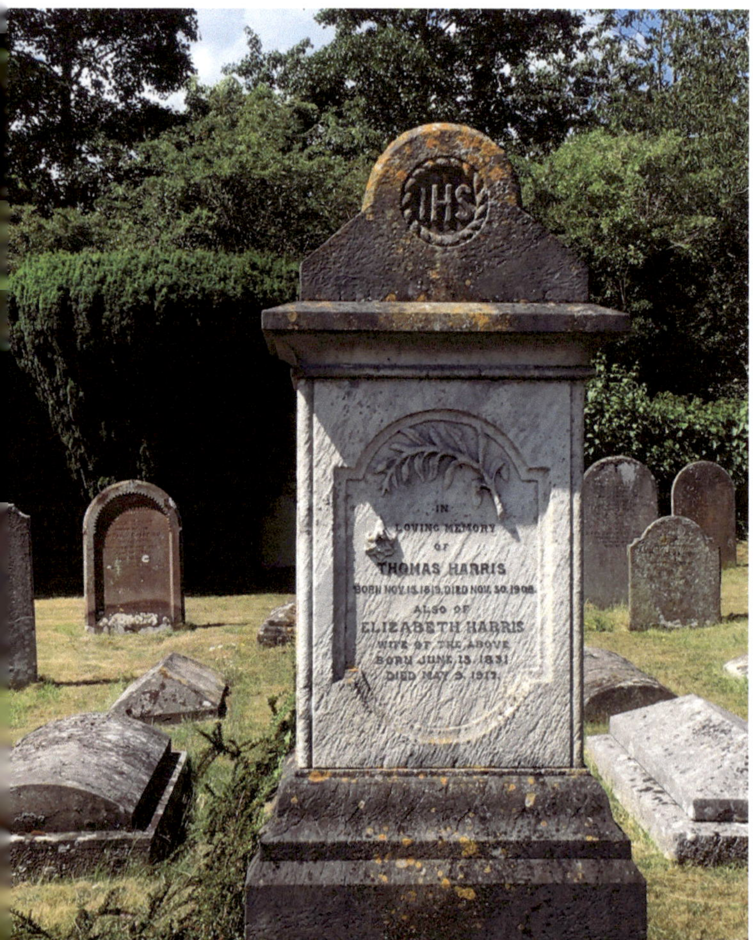

Grave of Thomas Harris, Curzon Street Cemetery. Obituary headline: 'Mr Thomas Harris, JP. Well known Calne citizen, a veteran Liberal, great philanthropist, five times Calne Mayor.' *Swindon Advertiser and North Wilts Chronicle*, 4 December 1908. (Author)

that the site was donated, and that an additional £500 was collected and invested in an endowment fund for future expenses. Thomas Harris agreed to donate £400, part of which was a gift of a piece of land he owned in New Road. It was opened 25 March 1905 by the Earl of Kerry.

Two Pigs, Phelps Parade, 1979 and 2017

The bronze sculpture by Calne artist Richard Cowdy was commissioned by Calne Civic Society, and unveiled by Lady Lansdowne in July 1979. On 1 October 2017, *Two Pigs* was stolen. Thanks to over 100,000 people taking to social media about the loss, it reached national TV news. Within three days, the *Two Pigs* was found, returned by Wiltshire Police, damage repaired by Andrew Blackford – thanks to the generosity of Calne Lions – and reinstalled. It was unveiled by Mayor Cllr Tony Trotman on 10 November 2017.

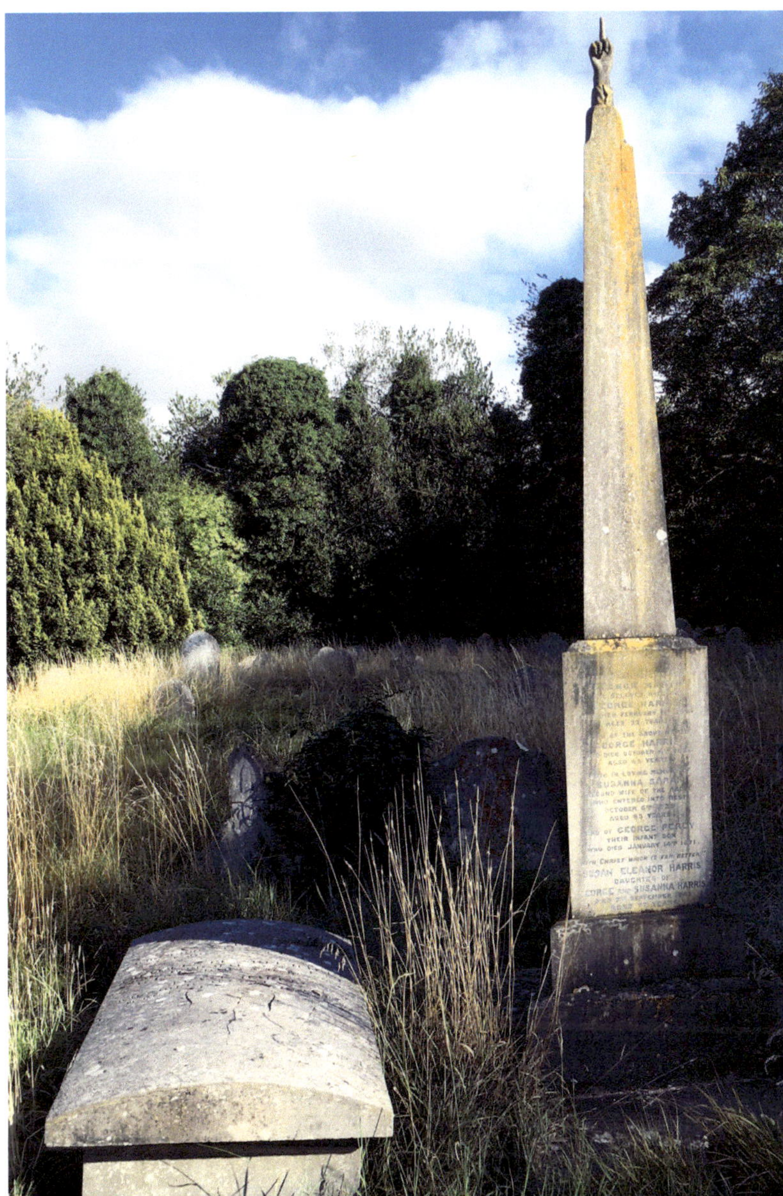

Holy Trinity churchyard. George Harris and family buried (right), memorial obelisk with finger pointing to heaven. Brother Charles and family buried (left), plain raised ledger monument. (Author)

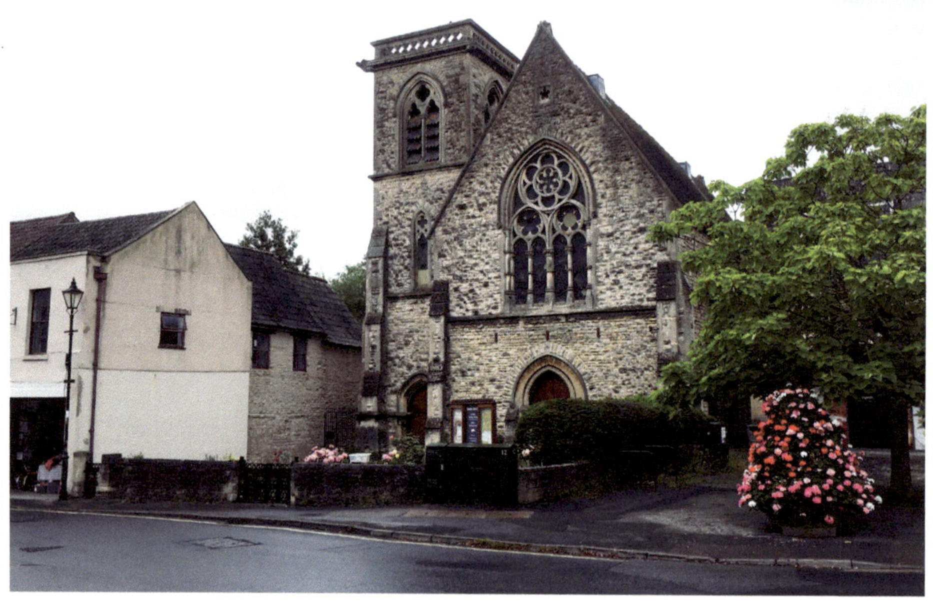

Calne Free Church was built 1867/8 on the site of the old Bear Inn, Church Street. It was designed by William J. Stent of Warminster. 'The bell tower has a quatrefoiled parapet with dragon gargoyles', 2020. (Author)

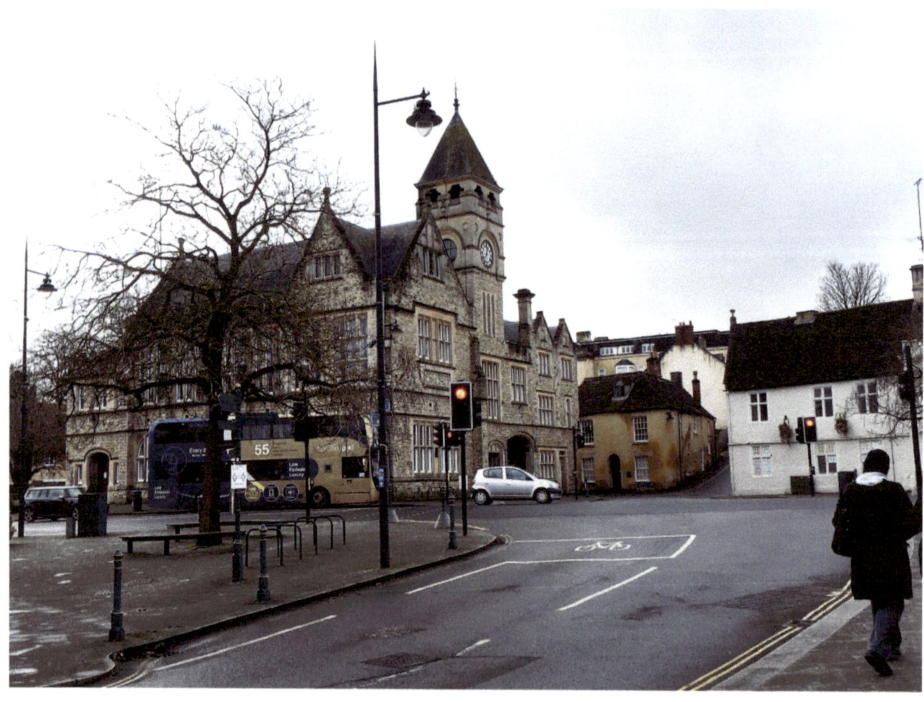

View of the Town Hall from Church Street, 2020. (Author)

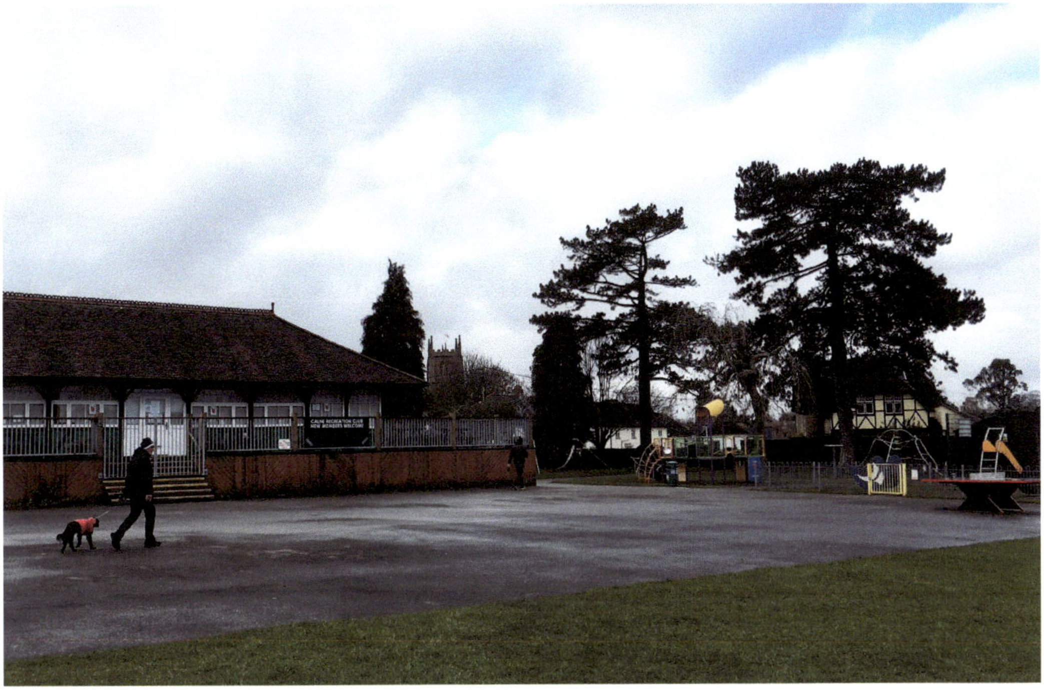

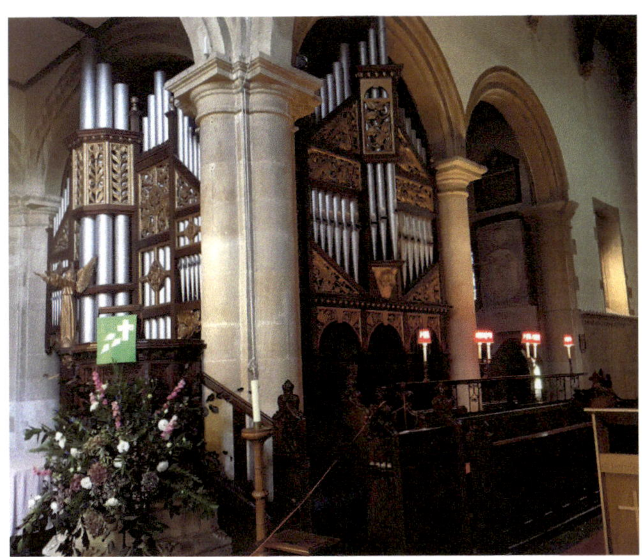

Calne Pavilion and Recreation Ground, Anchor Road, 2020. (Author)

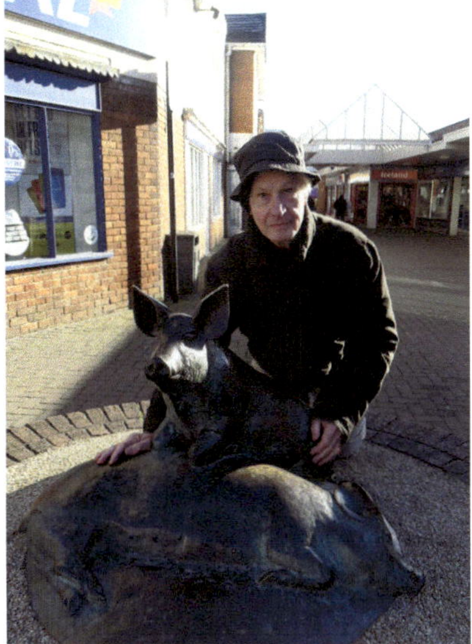

Above left: St Mary's Church organ was built in 1908 by master organ builder Peter Conacher of Huddersfield. The organ case was designed by C. R. Ashbee, leading figure in the Arts and Crafts movement. The Harris family paid the bill of £2,000. (Author)

Above right: Artist Richard Cowdy with his *Two Pigs*, Phelps Parade, 2021. The sculpture was made and cast in his own studio and bronze foundry in Calne. It was the first public work of art commissioned for the town in 1979. (Author)

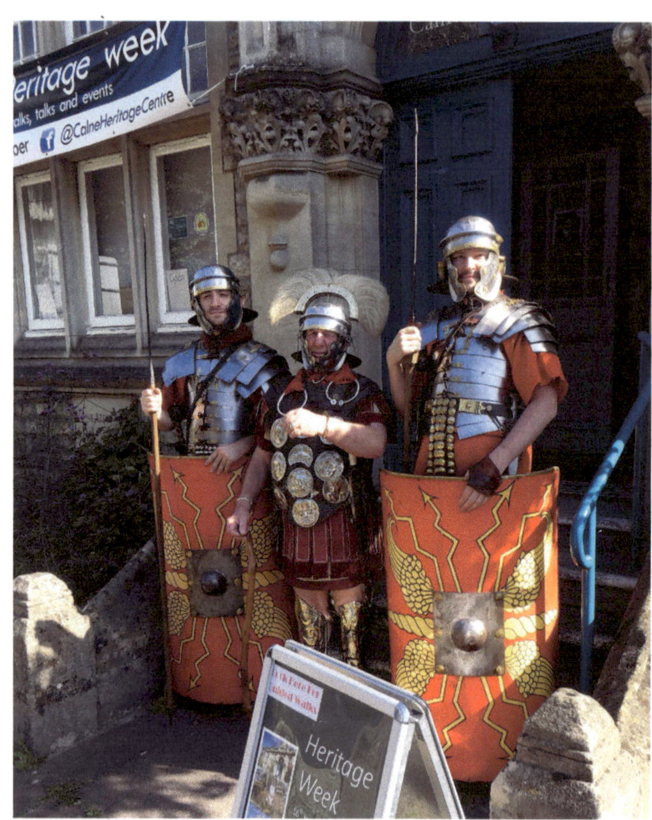

Left: Members of the Ermine Street Guard outside Calne Heritage Centre, formerly Carnegie Library, taking part in a Roman-themed day, Calne Heritage Week, 2019. (Author)

Below: Calne Camera Club recording the town's regeneration from St Mary's Church Tower, 1998. Left to right: Don Wallace, Sue Spearing, Don Lovelock, Maurice Hamblin, Mike Thomas, and David Webb (kneeling).

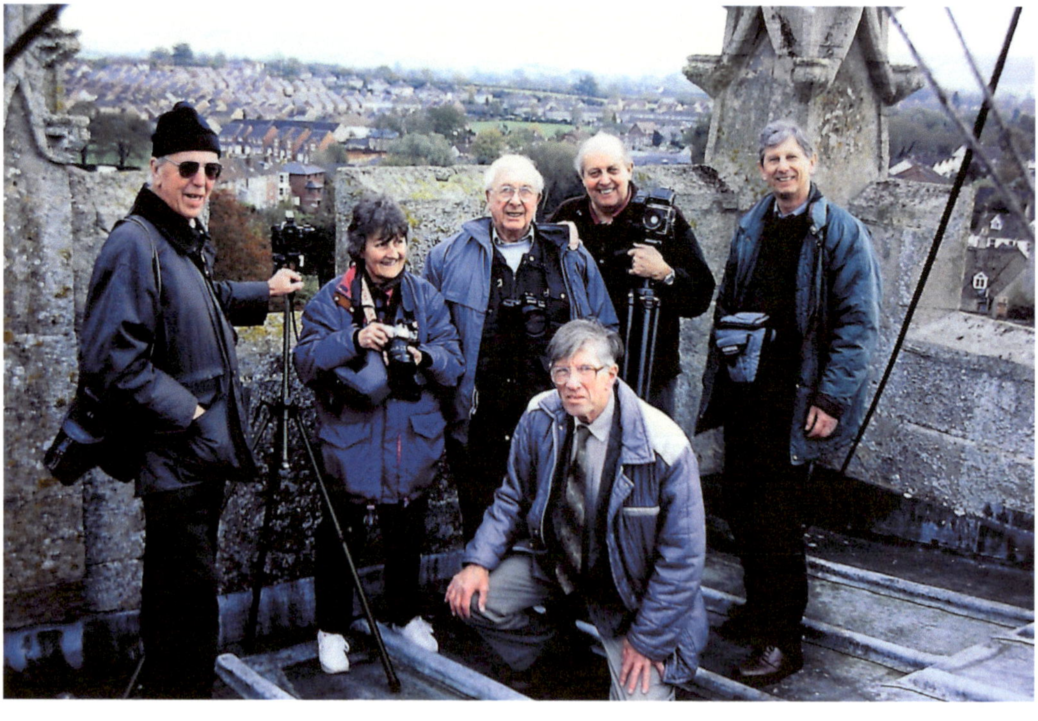

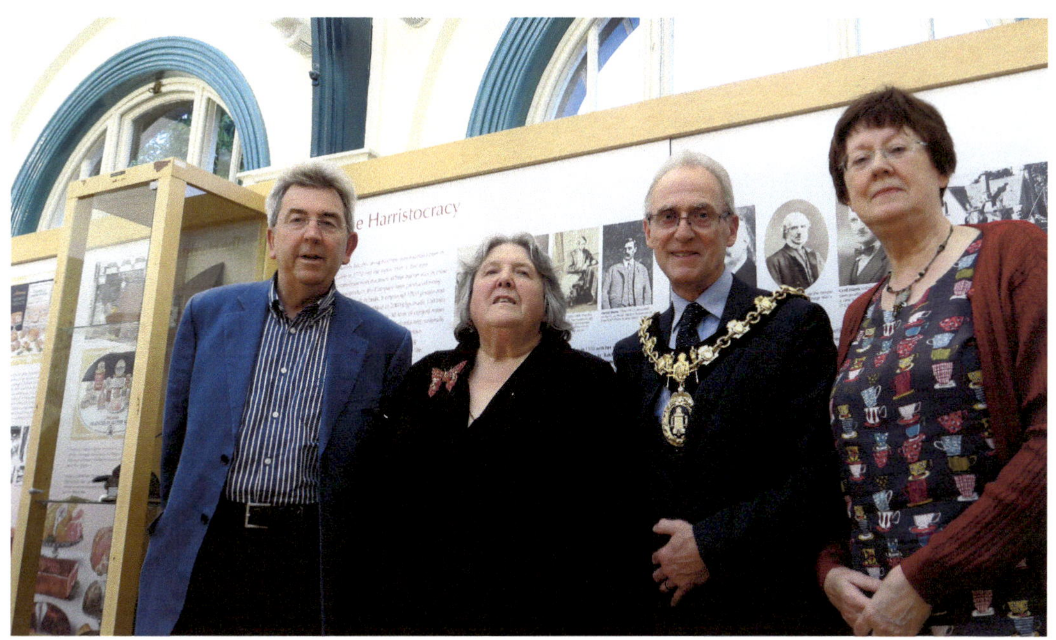

Left to right: Norman Beale, Sue Boddington, Mayor Cllr Tony Trotman and Dee La Vardera, four members of the Board of Trustees of Calne Heritage Centre, at the launch of new display boards, 2017. (Alfred La Vardera)

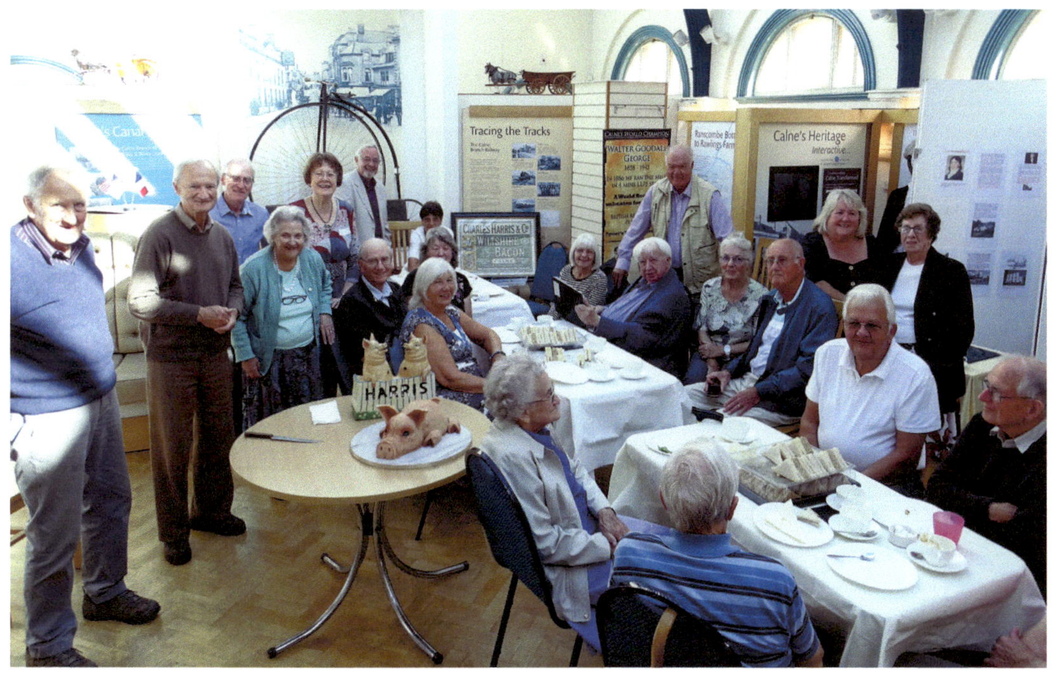

Harris's Reunion Tea Party, Calne Heritage Centre, 2019. Second from the left, David Harris (great-great-grandson of Charles Harris), member of the Board of Trustees, was invited to cut the celebration pig-shaped cake. (Tim Havenith)

12

A Different Kind of Legacy

'Being in good work – having a safe and secure job – is better for
your health than being out of work.'
Health Matters, Public Health England, 2020.

The Calne Study

Readers may be interested to know that there was an unexpected and very different legacy that arose from the closure of Harris's factory in 1982.

One of the town's general practitioners, Dr Norman Beale, saw the opportunity, about two years later, to perform what sociologists call a 'factory closure study'. He used the medical records (coded for anonymity) of his group practice at Calne Health Centre to follow the use of health services by the large number of registered patients who had also been long-standing employees at the factory.

He was then able to compare the numbers of doctor/patient interactions before and after redundancy. He was also able to examine data on close families and use a 'control group' – an equivalent number of otherwise comparable patients who worked elsewhere in Calne and who kept their jobs throughout the study. Recruiting the help of local mathematics teacher and statistician Susan Nethercott, Dr Beale compared patient consultation rates and referrals to hospital rates for years either side of July 1982 when the factory closed, and all the workers were made redundant.

At first, the results were inconclusive: there were no discernible differences in health service contacts before and after job loss. However, Dr Beale suddenly saw that there were consistent changes in patient demand – a jump in illnesses in his study group – around the time that the Harris workforce had been confronted by an earlier mass redundancy, in June 1980.

New analyses of the numbers showed that the changes coinciding with that event were statistically significant – that they could not have happened by chance. Here, for the very first time, was evidence of the true nature of 'unemployment morbidity' – that it begins when workers develop feelings of job insecurity rather than when they are actually 'thrown on the scrapheap'.

The ground-breaking findings were a political hot potato when national unemployment totals were in the millions, and the media soon took an interest.

After the first 'Beale and Nethercott' scientific paper was published in a reputable medical journal in November 1985, Dr Beale appeared on national news bulletins, in all the daily press, on breakfast television, regional magazine programmes, and even *The Jimmy Young Show* – a popular Radio 2 music and current affairs programme. A few months' later, he took a few days' leave to appear in a thirty-minute documentary produced by Granada Television's *World in Action,* in which many of the (very surprised) ex-Harris workers featured.

'The Calne Study' of health and unemployment has become very well known in academic circles. Dr Beale was awarded a prize by Cambridge University for the MD thesis he submitted, and the annual prize for research in general practice from the Royal College of General Practitioners where he was made a fellow. A leading article in *The British Medical Journal* on 16 March 1991 highlighted the main findings of the study:

> The study of Beale and Nethercott of redundancy in a meat factory has come to further fruition, building on the original findings that men and women and their families threatened with redundancy increased consultation rates by 20% and outpatient hospital visits by 60% compared with controls. They have now shown that many of the increased consultations resulted from chronic conditions (requiring treatment for over one year) which were six times more common among the unemployed. Cardiovascular disorders were particularly common among the unemployed men. In a follow-up study, men who remained unemployed were consulting general practitioners 57% more often about 13% more illnesses, were referred to hospital outpatient departments 80% more often and visited hospital twice as often. These results fit with data from the General Household Survey.

The Harris Factory findings still receive attention and young doctors training for general practice are introduced to 'The Calne Study'. They are reminded that research performed by general practitioners in their communities can make valuable contributions to medical knowledge. But more important, perhaps, is the insight they gain: that during consultations with their patients they must never forget to probe gently the topic of job security when no coherent diagnosis seems to fit the presenting symptoms or the patient is diffident to talk.

None of this helped, in any practical way, the 400 Harris employees who lost their livelihoods in 1982. It might console them to know that their experiences have led us all to a better understanding of the toxicity of enforced job loss.

C. & T. Harris (Calne) Ltd has become, if anything, more famous after its closure, and, one might say, that Dr Beale continued working there, even after the demolition of the buildings.

Afterword

The factories are long gone and production lines a distant memory but the market for pork products has not diminished. Pigs in blankets are not just for Christmas nor rashers of bacon just for breakfast. It may not be the Harris brand we eat now but the bacon is just as tasty, thanks to the pioneering work in bacon curing, which began in a small butcher's shop in Calne, Wiltshire, 250 years ago.

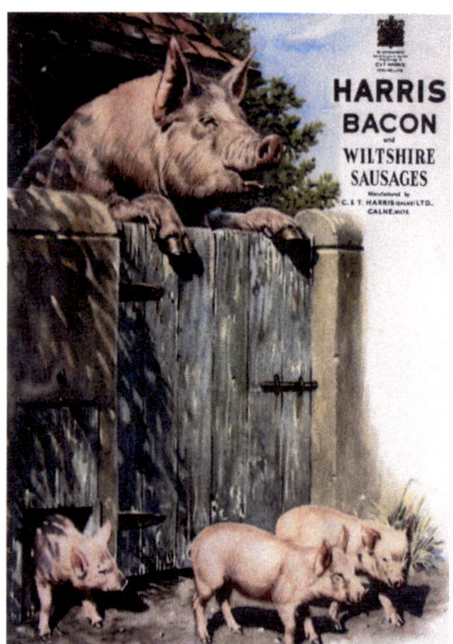

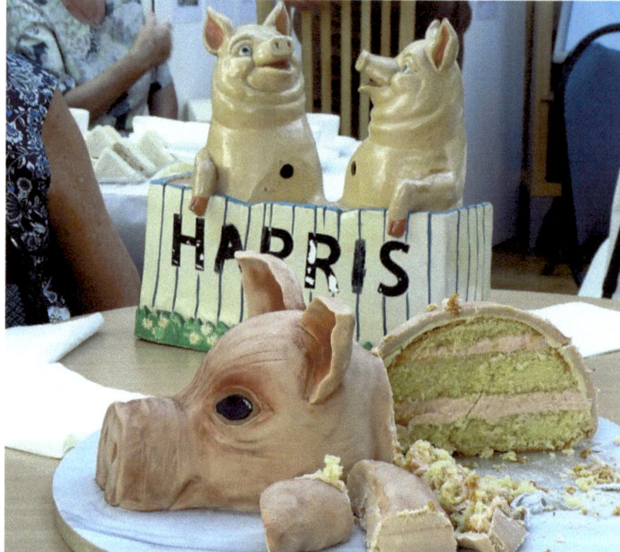

Above left: Happy Harris sow and piglets, 1890s design.

Above right: 250th anniversary cake made by Flying Pig Cake Emporium, Church Street, for Harris's Reunion Tea Party, 2019. (Tim Havenith)

Bibliography

Beale, N., *Is that the Doctor?* (1998)

Blackford & Son, *A Half-century and More of Building* (1939)

Boddington, S., *A Source of Pride: A Brief History of Calne Library* (WCC Library & Museum Service)

Bromham, J., *The History of C. & T. Harris* (1985); *Memoirs of a Small Town Man* (1989).

Calne Conservation Area Statement (with Calne Project, Calne Heritage Group, Calne Artists et al, NWDC, 1993)

Cooper, H., *History of the Harris Family at Calne, 1775–1907, With an Account of the Origin and Growth of their Bacon Curing Business in that Town* (1907)

Goddard, M., 'C. & T. Harris & Co. of Wiltshire', *Road Locomotive Society Journal,* February 2019

Havenith, T., *Calne Place Names* (Amazon, 2020)

Kelly's Directories

La Vardera, D., *Calne Living Memories* (Frith Book Company, 2004); *Bringing Home the Bacon* (Dewfall-hawk Press, 2018)

Maggs, C. G., *The Calne Branch* (Wild Swan, 1990)

Marsh, A. E. W., *A History of the Borough and Town of Calne* (Robert S Heath, Calne, 1903)

Power and Works Engineering Journal, March 1956

Tanner, G. H. J., *The Calne Branch,* (Oxford Publishing Co., 1972)

Telling Calne's Story (Centre for Environmental Interpretation, Manchester Polytechnic, 1991)

Treloar, P., *Calne in Camera* (Calne Town Council,1974); *Calne in Focus* (Calne Town Council, 1984); *Calne Revisited* (Calne Town Council, 1999); *Calne's Heritage* (The History Press, 2010)

Online Sources

British History Online: https://www.british-history.ac.uk/vch/wilts/vol17

British Listed Buildings: https://britishlistedbuildings.co.uk/

British Newspaper Archive: https://www.britishnewspaperarchive.co.uk

Currency converter: https://www.in2013dollars.com/uk/inflation/1888?amount=50

Government Guidance for Abattoirs: https://www.gov.uk/guidance/the-pig-carcase-grading-scheme-dress-and-grade-carcases

Grace's Guide to British Industrial History: https://gracesguide.co.uk

Number plate check: https://h2g2.com/entry/A4171114

Wiltshire Community History Census, Wiltshire Council: https://history.wiltshire.gov.uk/community/census_search2.php

Acknowledgements

Photographs, postcards, and newspaper cuttings albums donated to Calne Heritage Centre include those from the Baggs family, Blackford & Son, Calne Civic Society, Calne Project, Calne Town Council, Frank Dunlop, Jim Dunsford, B. F. Hacker, Don Haddrell, Ben Johnson, Don Lovelock and Peter Treloar.

Other photographs courtesy of Calne Camera Club, Dave Edwards, Julie Edwards, Marc Harding, Tim Havenith, Chris Hughes, Eddy Lane, Dee La Vardera, Roger Onslow, Michael Thomas, Susan Waite, Michael Wiggins and Wiltshire & Swindon History Centre.

Thanks to Norman Beale, Michael Bennett, Andrew Blackford, Sue Boddington, Robert Bromham, David Harris, Tim Havenith, Andrew Spearey, Edward Spearey, Steven Thomas, Tony Trotman, and Mike White for their time and knowledge.

Also, to Mary-Ann Angell, Tim Buckeridge, Ken Hulbert, Garry Hunt, Kate Jenks, Bob Lawrence, Audrey Lucas, Christine Pottow, Rod Pottow, Brian Provis, Barbara Sealy, Doug Smart, Dave Stone, Sheila Thornton, Clive Van Hoek, Joe Watkins, Ian Wiggins and Sheila Woodman.

Many thanks to members of Calne in Photographs Facebook group, who shared memories of life at C. & T. Harris (Calne) Ltd.

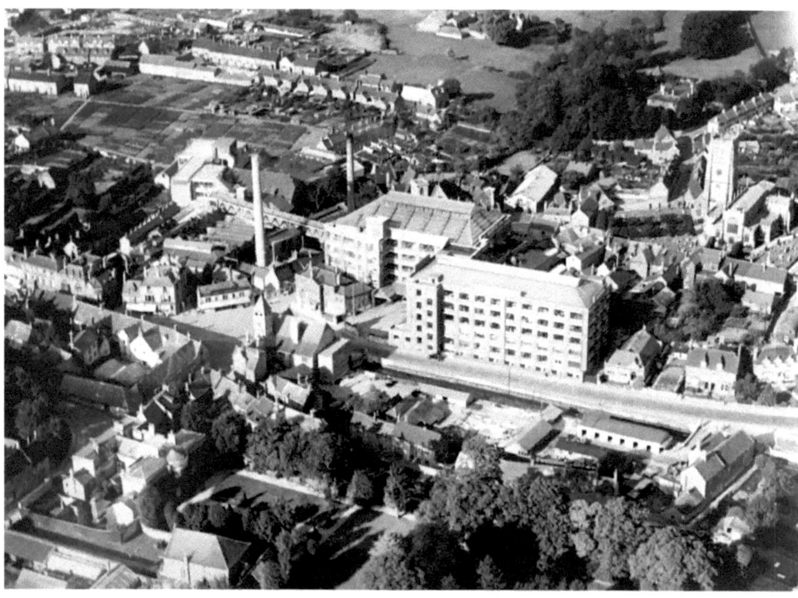

Aerial view of Calne, *c.* 1935.